how to **design a successful**

petrol station

a note of thanks...

The easiest and by far the most enjoyable part of any book is to write the note of thanks!

It is with great pride that I can thank my close collaborators at Minale Tattersfield Design Strategy. Without their skill in designing successful petrol stations, this book would never have been possible.

But I would like to give a special thanks to Lucy Hughes who collected the material and interviewed the relevant designers, architects and clients to put together the story behind each project; David Davis, our creative director and a man from whom I have learnt an awful lot. He has an intuitive vision for the end product which is second to none; Rosie Smith, one of our talented young graphic designers who has stoically played the carrot and stick game with me - "Yes, I like what you have done, but can you do it again!" "This is much better. It is brilliant, but can you change it to this."

I would also like to thank Peter Brown and Sam Hampton for helping to visualise the station of the future, and my son Marcello Mario for designing the perfect book jacket.

Thank you to all our contributors and in particular Paddy Briggs for his foreword and his support in supplying information on Shell.

And finally let me thank James and Edward Booth-Clibborn, my publishers, who foolishly continue to believe in my books.

Marcello Minale

Minale Tattersfield Design Strategy: European partners conference in Richmond, Surrey

EDITORS

Marcello Minale & Edward Booth-Clibborn

ART DIRECTION

Marcello Minale

BOOK DESIGN

Rosie Smith & Robin Chapman

BOOK JACKET DESIGN

Marcello Mario Minale

TEXT

Lucy Hughes & Marcello Minale

PRINTERS

Dai Nippon Printing

DISTRIBUTORS
UK & WORLDWIDE

Internos Books
12 Percy Street London W1P 9FB
Tel: (020) 7637 4255 Fax: (020) 7637 4251

ITALY

Ulrico Hoepli Editore Spa.
20121 Milano Via Hoepli 5
Tel: (02) 86 48 71 Fax: (02) 805 2886

Since this book was first conceived, the design companies responsible for the original designs may have ceased to trade, changed their name or merged with another company. To avoid confusion, the credit has been given to the original company that undertook the work, for this is where the design expertise for each specific project lies.

Edward Booth-Clibborn
Editor

CONTENTS

01

foreword by Paddy Briggs

introduction by Marcello Minale

FOREWORD BY PADDY BRIGGS
Manager for Shell's Retail Visual Identity project, 1990-1995

"Between two products equal in price, function and quality, the better looking will outsell the other."

Raymond Loewy

Whilst the history of brands goes back more than one hundred years, brand differentiation as a marketing tool for global businesses only really took off in the last quarter of the twentieth century. A key element of this brand differentiation in nearly all product and service categories is design. Raymond Loewy, designer of the latest variant of the Shell emblem (the "Pecten") and one of the all time greats of the design world, knew what the game was all about. The good marketeer seeks to differentiate his product to achieve consumer preference in every way that he can. But where the product or service is very similar between competing brands, the brand that looks better will outsell the others.

Petroleum products retailing is often perceived as a commodity activity. Certainly the fuel that is dispensed into your car is unlikely to vary greatly between the principal suppliers. When an innovation does occur (new additives for example), most of the major players are likely to be able to offer similar performance advantages. So when the basic product is broadly similar, companies must compete in other areas if they are to achieve competitive advantage. In the past the network was everything. The company with the most sites in the best locations would lead the way. To an extent this is still true, but the advent of hypermarkets, which not only offer low prices but also have strong generic retail brands behind them eg Carrefour, Sainsbury's), has radically changed the competitive scene in many countries.

So with products being broadly similar, with network development somewhat less important and with powerful new players on the scene the oil companies have been forced to innovate in other areas if they are to avoid the spiral into price wars, vanishing margins and commodity retailing. Design is one of the weapons in the hands of the companies, something that Shell realised back in 1989 when the genesis of the Retail Visual Identity (RVI) project, for which I was the project manager, began.

However, by the end of the 1980s the opportunity to use design as a differentiating tool for the Shell brand began to gather favour, both in Shell International and in many of the more than 120 Shell companies around the world where Shell had branded retail operations. This was partly a response to competition (BP was the first global innovator) and partly a growing realisation that focusing on the molecules (the mixture that made up fuels products) was unlikely to be a source of genuine competitive advantage except in a few niche areas. In addition, in many markets there was much tighter control of the network (many more sites were owned by Shell rather than by independent dealers, for example). The RVI project was a response to all this.

Shell and other oil companies were rather slow to respond to the retail revolution of the 1980s. The consumer experience in most other retail categories during these years became better and brighter, far more comfortable and with much greater functionality - but generally retail petrol stations lagged behind. This was ironic in a way because the multinational oil companies were by far the biggest global branded retailers (Shell had nearly 50,000 sites world-wide compared with McDonalds' 14,000 in 1990). Furthermore, fuel purchase for the car is one of the most frequent repeat buying activities for consumers (averaging at least once a week in many markets).

In the past oil company management often had a producer logic rather than a consumer pull imperative. I remember one Shell company in which I worked where the Chief Executive, a geologist, used to refer to marketing as "disposal". The idea of satisfying consumer needs was an alien concept to him - he was not alone! In addition to this bias there was also the problem that oil companies did not always control tightly the channel in which their products were sold. In many markets the petrol station was run by independent dealers and the oil company could only exercise a limited degree of control over the appearance of the site and the nature of the service on it.

From the start the RVI project was not about cosmetics. The motorist is not a fool and he (and increasingly she) is not going to be taken in by design changes alone, however elegant. The designers who worked on RVI knew this well and throughout the design development we worked with them to improve functionality and comfort, as well as appearance. This meant that the emphasis on site shifted from "product" to "convenience". At every stage in the design development we were trying to make the refuelling experience on Shell sites more agreeable for the motorist. Coincidentally, at the same time the growth of shops and convenience stores on our sites was gathering pace. So the "c-store option" was designed into RVI from the start. But as well as offering more on the site in the way of grocery items etc, there was also the recognition that the primary purpose of the site would always be to dispense vehicle fuels. The challenge was to make this task as simple, convenient and stress-free as possible.

Research told us that major improvements were necessary to the generic petrol station if the consumer was always to feel comfortable when visiting. Clear signage; ease of use of equipment; well illuminated forecourts; clean and accessible lavatories; easy payment procedures and many more elements were seen to be important in all of the more than twenty countries where we did extensive market research. This led to key elements of the RVI design such as innovative under-canopy lighting systems; clear and readable graphics on signs, and a generally uncluttered forecourt. But the "emotional" aspects of the design development were not missed either. By the careful use of colour, form, architectural elements, lighting etc we were able to create an environment that was not only more functional but also more pleasant and comfortable.

The consumer response to the RVI design, both in research and subsequently when motorists visited the new sites, was very encouraging. Shell's competitive position was significantly enhanced as RVI was introduced and our financial performance improved. So Raymond Loewy would today be proud to know that his wise words have another category where they strongly apply.

I hope that the publication of this splendid book will keep the subject of petrol station design high on the oil marketeers' agenda and that top designers, like Marcello Minale and David Davis, will continue to try and push us in new directions so that we surprise and delight our customers even more in the future!

Paddy Briggs

Dubai, May 2000

INTRODUCTION BY MARCELLO MINALE
so why have I decided to write this book?

Having worked in the design industry for over 30 years, designing petrol stations among other things, I have never found a reference book which could give me any hints on how to do it.

I think that it is true to say that we all belong to the petrol station generation. They have always played a part in our lives. And over the years, as the car has evolved, our lives have developed in parallel. But while the car has changed dramatically from the first Ford A, the distribution of its fuel has not.

The station that inspired us to design the mobile petrol station!

Inspecting an uncladded petrol pump at the Gilbarco factory before redesigning the panelling

As part of this exercise I have decided to reconstruct various steps in the evolution of the petrol station. Notably, very little has changed since the first gas station was built in the United States around 1925. Indeed, if we take as an example Mobil's station designed by Chermayeff & Geismar and built in the early 1970s, it is interesting to note the striking similarities between this and the latest station designed by Norman Foster for Repsol.

However, both fall into the same trap. The Mobil design, though innovative, proved expensive to reproduce and was ultimately dropped. The Norman Foster design, I believe, will follow suit, unless it has been designed as a flagship station - an architectural statement not to be rolled out across the network.

At Minale Tattersfield Design Strategy we aim to produce designs that work. Since an important consideration for many petrol retailers is the size of their networks (Shell 50,000, BP 15,000, AGIP 15,000 and Total 10,000), cost is clearly a key factor and designs need to be practical. For this reason, an individual architectural gesture is very difficult to achieve across a whole network. What's more, historically companies who have pursued this route have had to abandon it. Many of us will remember the pre-stressed concrete which littered Europe. In the end these stations proved too difficult to build, too expensive to apply the company image to and then too expensive to knock down.

In this book I have only included forecourt designs which I believe have made a contribution to the evolution of the petrol station. You will notice some notable omissions such as petrol giant, Esso. The reason for this is that, in my opinion, they have employed only superficial measures to update their retail network and have made no impact on the future development of forecourt design.

Petrol station livery panels at the Gilbarco factory, ready to be assembled on petrol pumps

Two dramatic stations - Eppco designed by Landor and Emarat designed by Wolff Olins

architectural evolution of the petrol station - depiction of styles through the ages

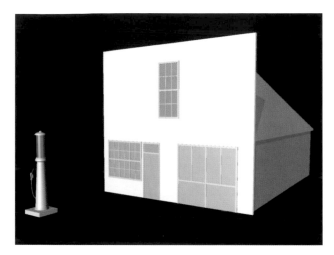

1920 Barn

1920 Arches

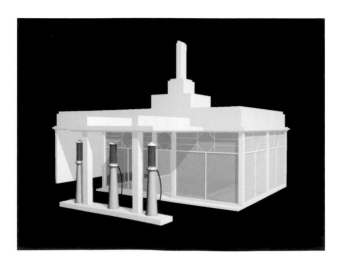

1935 Deco

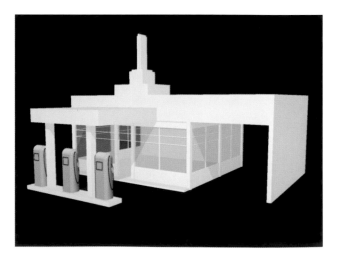

1935 Constructivist

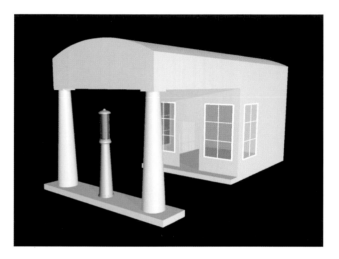

1925 Columns

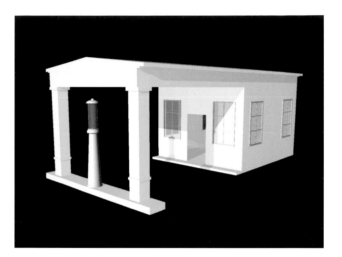

1930 Palladium

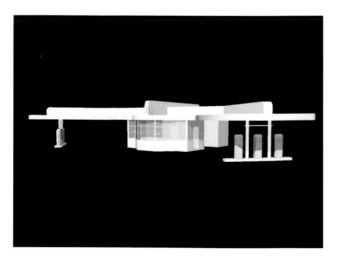

1936 Twin

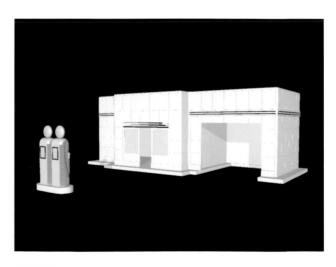

1940 Tiled

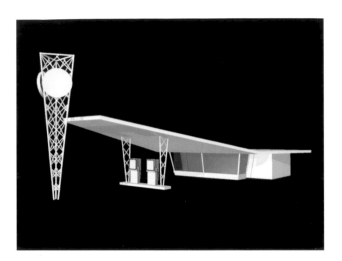

1960 Angled

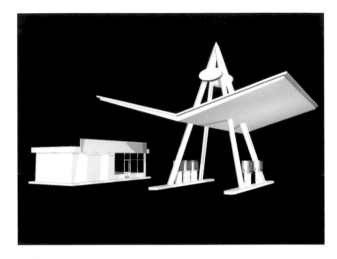

1962 Inverted V

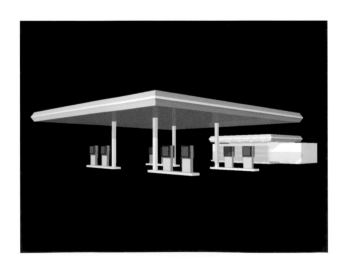

1970 Angled nosing

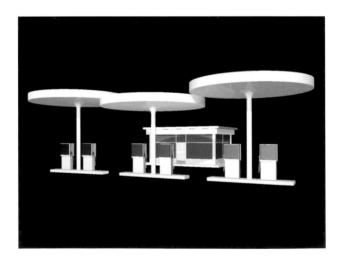

1970 Mushrooms

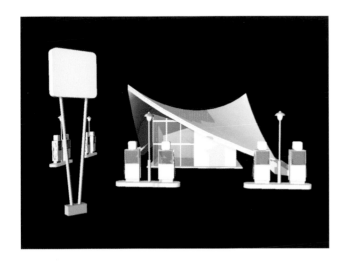

1963 Batwing

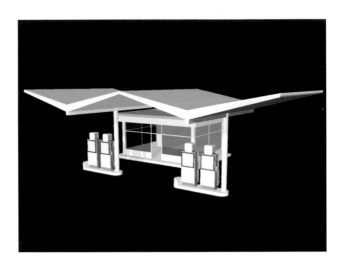

1970 V wing

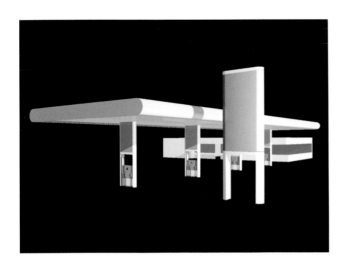

1989 Curved nosing

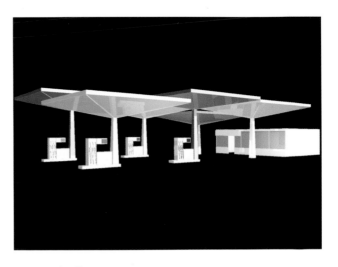

2000 Umbrellas

The Americans developed the concept of the modern petrol station comprising four simple steel supports and a canopy. All evolution that has happened since has been based on this formula.

When we look at recent developments in forecourt design we cannot ignore the important part that the material Alucabond has played. It is this that has facilitated the production of straight lines on a large scale. I have always said that it is easier to send man to the moon than to create a straight line and it is here that the success of the BP retrofit system lies. For the first time it was possible to apply a curved fascia in a straight line, to project an image of quality and modernity.

So, who are the people who can design petrol stations? In my opinion architects are not the best people since they lean towards grandiose statements not suited to a large-scale roll out. There are few consultancies which have developed the skill that combines brand identity, graphics, industrial design, landscape design, retail design, signage and most recently, multimedia design.

Obviously, the petrol station has evolved to a degree, but mainly in terms of size. The first petrol station was an extension of the grocery store and today it has become the grocery store itself.

The big revolution will come with the advent of e-commerce. In this introduction and in a lecture I gave at OPAL's conference on "The e-commerce challenge" in May 2000, I have attempted to predict the petrol station of the future. I believe the petrol station will become a central point where purchases ordered over the internet can be delivered and picked up. With the explosion of e-commerce we run the risk of severe congestion on our roads as hundreds of white vans deliver goods to millions of households across the country. With an extensive network of petrol stations already in place across the country, the infrastructure is in place to alleviate this problem. What's more, it makes sense as a time-saving device since the purchases can be loaded straight into the car as it is filled up with petrol or its battery is recharged.

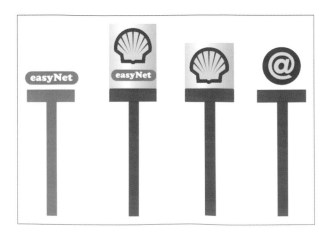

Possible signage for a 'cyber-site'

Minale Tattersfield's proposal for the e-commerce petrol station of the future

Over the years, we at Minale Tattersfield Design Strategy have developed a transportable petrol station, a suspended petrol pump, the concept of advertising on the under canopy, drive-thru banking, video distribution, the internet café and the solar panelled station, but nothing will compare to the e-commerce revolution. From now on we need to think differently about how we dispense energy and exploit the potential herein to dramatically change the way we lead our lives on a daily basis.

Marcello Minale

Richmond, May 2000

GETTING DESIGNS ON THE FUTURE...

a vision beyond the auto-centric world by Marcello Minale

From a lecture given at the third annual conference for Marketing Week:
Meeting the Next Challenge in Petrol Forecourt Marketing, May 2000

Over the years the petrol station has become an institution. Romanticised in the paintings of Edward Hopper and providing the set in films and plays, the petrol station has become an unavoidable factor in most people's daily lives. Yet with all the technological advances in the petroleum industry as a whole, it is notable how the petrol forecourt remains relatively unchanged from the early days. In fact it would be fair to say that petrol retailing has come full circle.

Petrol retailing began in the United States around the turn of the century. By 1910 the principles of modern underground storage with pump and hose dispensing had been developed and curb pumps began to appear on the streets of every city and town in the US. This soon began to cause congestion in the streets and in 1913 the Gulf Oil company opened the first petrol station built for the purpose with off-street fuelling - the first true forerunner of the roadside petrol station as we know it today. By 1915 the concept of branded gasoline was beginning to appear with names such as "Good Gulf Gasoline" and "The Texas Company Filling Station".

A significant development came in 1928 when Totem Ice Stores teamed up with Transcontinental Oil to locate a number of Transcontinental's petrol stations adjacent to Totem Ice Stores creating the first petrol/convenience store tie-in. This would prove a thriving relationship and one which I believe is crucial in today's market. Convenience stores and grocers around the country began to provide customers with refuelling facilities as an additional service. Over the years we see the emphasis gradually shift from fuel being offered at grocery stores as an added extra, to stores which are gasoline based with store sales as a secondary function. Now in the UK we are reverting to the original situation with a greater emphasis on store sales since this is where the larger profit margins lie today.

Early petrol station, 1925, dual-branded Richfield/Pan-Gas

Early curb-side Shell Station, 1930

Gilmore station 1935, not dissimilar to a contemporary forecourt

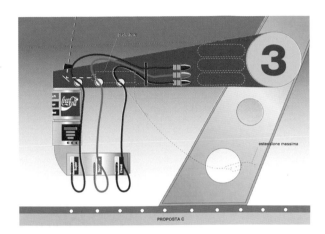

Suspended pump

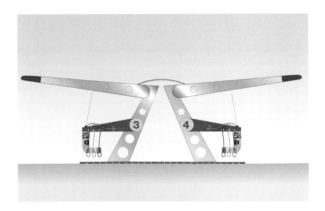

Wing station with suspended pumps

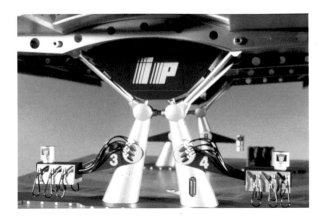

Canopy structure and suspended pumps

But first let's take a look at the design of the petrol forecourt. As previously mentioned, visually the forecourt remains relatively unchanged from the first purpose-built off-road gas stations. Petrol stations may have increased in size with more pumps offering a greater choice in fuel, but overall there are still many similarities to be drawn between the gas stations depicted in the paintings of Edward Hopper and those of today. All this could change, however, with the introduction of a suspended petrol pump developed by Minale Tattersfield Design Strategy. This mechanism has been designed not only to revolutionise the appearance of the traditional petrol station forecourt but to tackle the problems of pollution caused by leaks from the pump itself.

This simple structure has a number of notable advantages. With no direct contact to the ground leaks are less likely to occur and are easier to detect. Drips from the nozzle which inevitably occur are easily cleaned reducing the release of harmful gases into the atmosphere and petrol is less likely to seep into the ground. It is also easier to maintain. Instead of the operational mechanics being concentrated in the comparatively small body of the old pump, they are spread across a wider area and are easier to access. Leaks in the pipes are equally easy to detect.

Using the suspended pump the appearance of the station forecourt is transformed. The range of view is not restricted by the old style pumps. This improved visibility enables motorists to locate free pumps immediately, ensuring the free flow of traffic. It also helps the service station attendant to identify any security risk and raise the alarm. Aesthetically, the suspension of the pumps creates a cleaner, lighter and less cluttered environment.

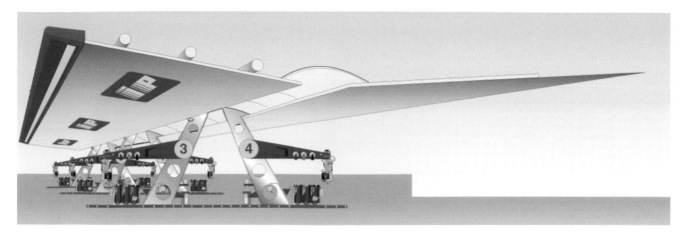

This canopy structure provides advertising opportunities

The structure of the suspended pump has created numerous possibilities for a revolutionary kind of station decoration. The canopy structure affords advertising opportunities or an area to display works of art. It would be equally feasible to attach large video screens which would increase revenue and make the mundane task of filling the car a pleasure as opposed to a chore.

Minale Tattersfield is continually working on new concepts which could potentially revolutionise petrol retailing. Another such concept is the G3 transportable petrol station. This was conceived by Minale while on a trip to Russia. He saw that people were driving miles to refuel and felt that an innovative concept was needed to address the problem.

This concept is discussed in greater detail in the Mintat G3 chapter (chapter 15 page 216).

So where does the future of forecourt retailing lie today? For some time large supermarket chains have been encroaching on the territory traditionally dominated by oil companies, constructing their own petrol stations and selling fuel at competitive prices. Increased competition has meant that the profit margins involved in petrol retailing have been greatly reduced and as a reaction petrol companies have turned to food retailing.

The Mintat G3 transportable petrol station

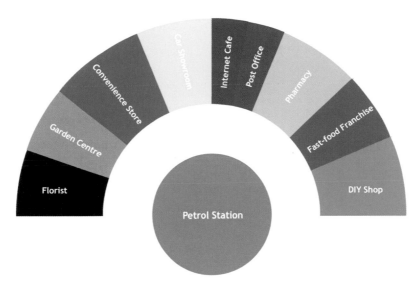

Minale's vision for a retail village focused around a petrol station forecourt

To capitalise on this change in focus from petrol retailing to the more profitable convenience store, Minale Tattersfield has developed a new retail concept for IP (Italiana Petroli). IP Planet is currently being tested in a number of stations across Italy. The concept comprises an in-store banking service, parcel post, video rental, lottery and touch-screen information point. An additional internet café could also be included in larger station forecourts.

Another concept devised by Minale Tattersfield takes the tie-up between service station and convenience store one step further. It envisages a situation where a petrol station provides the focal point for a small retail 'village', providing essential services for the local community. A selection of shops such as a general store, post office and garden centre are built around a central petrol station. This has the advantage of easy access and for heavy purchases from the garden centre or DIY shop, the car is close at hand. A drive-thru banking service could be incorporated to achieve optimum convenience for the customer.

This year saw the launch by Shell of a new pilot scheme - a petrol station which unusually does not sell petrol. Whether this idea will catch on with other petrol retailers is as yet uncertain. But although Shell Select is the first store to stand alone, convenience stores are now a feature on every petrol station forecourt. It might not be long before the circle is completed and we return to the situation of the 1920s when grocery stores and drug stores also happened to sell a bit of petrol.

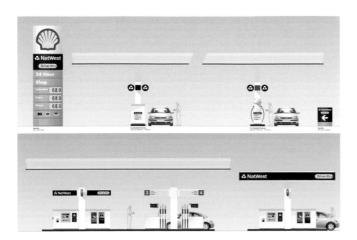

Concepts for a drive-thru bank

02

forecourt design by Addison, London
corporate identity by Siegel & Gale
packaging by Minale Tattersfield Design Strategy
exploratory concepts by Minale Tattersfield Design Strategy

BP

forecourt design by Addison, London
corporate identity by Siegel & Gale
packaging by Minale Tattersfield Design Strategy
exploratory concepts by Minale Tattersfield Design Strategy

BP logo

In 1987 British Petroleum was privatised. The decision had already been taken to update the station network to coincide with privatisation. The new image would represent BP's new, more dynamic approach to marketing and reflect its concern for environmental issues. The designs proved to be a huge success and BP became the leader of a revolution in petrol station design which was to sweep the industry. BP set a new standard in forecourt design and became the benchmark by which other petrol retailers began to measure themselves.

Prior to the implementation programme, BP's station design had been unexceptional - a generic station forecourt with a very weak application of the BP branding. It did little more than indicate the presence of a petrol station and failed to communicate anything positive about the BP brand. Since BP at this time was not a brand leader, it had little to lose in a radical approach to the redesign of its retail visual identity (in contrast to Shell, for example, which had well established, positive brand associations which it did not want to lose in adopting a radical new identity). Whereas Shell a few years later opted for an evolutionary approach to its redesign programme, BP could afford to be a little more adventurous and the road they took revolutionised the BP station network.

Detail of service area

Directional signage

BP began by analysing its existing identity to evaluate key brand equities which should be retained and optimised. Research revealed that although its brand image had begun to deteriorate, the green/yellow colour combination had strong positive associations with consumers and the shield symbol linked to the BP name suggested quality and reliability. Throughout the 80s, the consumer had grown increasingly sophisticated and had begun to have higher expectations of the retail environment. This change was most noticeable in the high street, but the inevitable spin-off meant that in comparison the image of the oil retailer was further undermined. BP needed little convincing that its new image needed to project a much higher level of quality and service to customers, since it was clear that petrol retailers were subject to the same market forces as all other retailers.

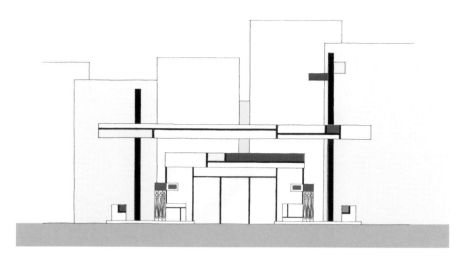

Mondrian design for BP urban petrol station, original proposal by Minale Tattersfield for BP, 1985

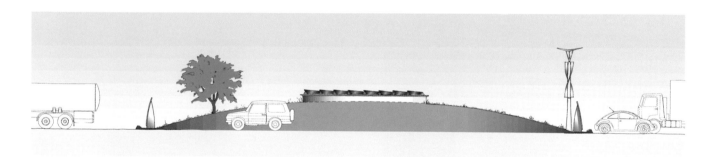

Minale Tattersfield's exterior view of an underground petrol station, suitable for locations of natural beauty, designed for BP, 1985

Section of station - a proposal for an underground petrol station by Minale Tattersfield for BP, 1985

Minale Tattersfield was initially approached to produce concepts for a new station forecourt. The designs produced were quite outrageous. The design proposal was divided in two - the urban station and the rural station.

In the urban station the BP identity was reduced to a minimum. The logo disappeared all together and instead it was replaced by a design in the style of Mondrian. It was Minale Tattersfield's belief that the consumer would soon associate any brightly painted station with BP. In the countryside the stations were to be located underground in order to preserve the natural environment. These were to be located by a simple roadside flag.

The proposals, which were intended to challenge preconceptions of the station forecourt, were well received. However, in the end BP opted for Addison, London's proposal to brand the station green.

Perhaps the most significant feature of the new image was the application of the BP branding in a three-dimensional format on all the main architectural elements such as the canopy and roadside signage. This has been a revolutionary step in an industry which had for decades been using two-dimensional decorative finishes. Following BP's redesign, it quickly became apparent that this very crude branding device did not convey the same level of quality as BP's use of form. And so BP became pioneers in the use of form as a differentiator with the vast majority of other retailers quickly following suit.

The logo was also adjusted for a more up-to-date appearance. The shield was retained but modernised and the letters were italicised, giving the appearance of a more professional operator.

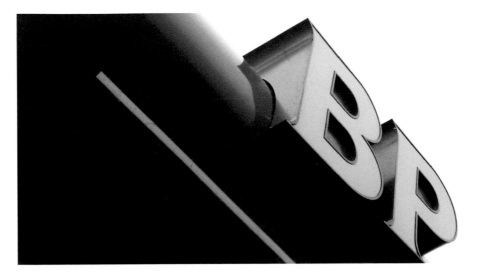

Detail of lettering

Petrol station and totem

Detail of totem

The shape of the shield is unique to BP and its curve influenced the architectural development, particularly the canopy. Alucabond was used to form the gentle curves of the canopy. Unlike vinyl and acrylic which let light pass through, this substance which consists of three layers (aluminium/polyethylene/aluminium) is opaque. This led to the development of a new lighting system. Simple but highly effective, a green neon strip is fixed below the canopy lip reflecting onto the curved surface above. The branding is clearly illuminated but the light is neither harsh nor cold.

A significant development was also made in the pump design. The column and pump signage has been incorporated into a single monolithic arrangement, which became known as the monocolumn. This has proved a very popular development, which has been used extensively throughout the industry ever since.

The new forecourt design was an immediate success and was rolled out across the network world-wide. The design was particularly popular in Australia where they see the green and yellow of BP as their unofficial national colours.

The colour green is the predominant colour in the new RVI. It has been used more extensively and applied consistently throughout. In this way it capitalises on the colour's positive associations with eco-friendly policies and supports BP's stance as an environmentally sensitive oil company. Both colours were specially specified for a more modern appearance and have been applied in a more extrovert and confident manner. When applied to a curved surface the green picks up the highlights and lowlights to dynamic effect, reminiscent of the way light plays on a car's paintwork. The curved surface of the canopy and colour work well together.

Today BP's RVI has become a powerful communication tool and the BP brand has come to represent modernity, professionalism, dynamism and care for the environment. The new forecourt design, which uses form in a meaningful way like a product or a car, was a very significant development in forecourt design world-wide and has set the trend ever since. It has succeeded in conveying a very high level of quality without sacrificing function.

The BP forecourt retail outlet - Express

In recent years, with the development of its own retail brand, BP has also been recognised as the pioneer of a new retail philosophy for petrol retailers. The BP Express brand was successfully launched across the world. It represented a tacit acknowledgement that though primarily retailers of petrol, they too had to conform to the retail standards consumers had come to expect.

BP has also continued to demonstrate its commitment to eco-friendly petrol retailing. It was the first company to use solar panels on the station canopy in any significant way. Today they continue to run a certain number of stations operating on solar energy alone.

packaging programme

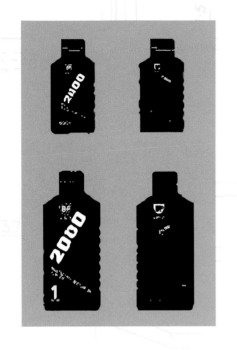

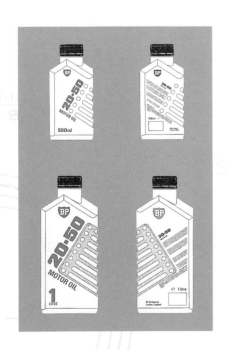

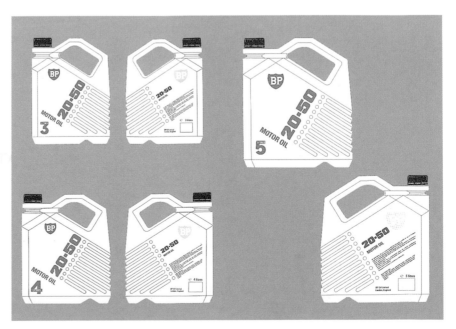

34

Final packaging design

Seven pictograms depicting the
particular use of each product

An early sketch for an advertising support

shelving display units for products

Mobile display unit

Central display stand, which can be accessed from all four sides

The prototype new build BP service station at Rushet, South West London

The new BP logo launched 25th July 2000, designed by Landor

Marcello Minale's comment

The BP station conceived 15 years ago represented the first step in the revolution of forecourt design. The use of alucabond (two sheets of aluminium with a plastic polyethylene core) played a major role. This lightweight material can be bent whilst at the same time maintaining a straight line. It is easier to send man to the moon than it is to produce a perfectly straight line.

Another key development has been the use of double columns which incorporate the pump in between. Since 1935 single columns had been used and those who had tried to escape the constraints these imposed (such as Mobil with their Umbrella Station) have all returned in the end.

After 15 years the BP station has clearly weathered well. It has been a leading reference point for other petrol retailers. The new look was completed with the upgrading of their lube oil packaging system. The convenience store concept has also been tackled well with the Express brand.

The merger of BP Amoco has resulted in a new symbol, strongly critised by the national press (Daily Telegraph 25th July 2000).

My personal comment is that BP had a chance to move towards the future, but with this new symbol they have made a significant step backwards.

03

designed by Addison, London
logo by Raymond Loewy International
visual identity manual by Sampson Tyrell

SHELL

designed by Addison, London
logo by Raymond Loewy International
visual identity manual designed by Sampson Tyrell

By the end of the 80s it had become clear that in order for Shell to retain its position as brand leader, a comprehensive review of its retail visual identity was required. In 1990 consumer research was conducted in 10 countries, which revealed two key findings. Firstly, while the Shell brand was considered by consumers as warm, friendly and reassuring it was also viewed as old fashioned. Secondly, it revealed that the petrol station forecourt was perceived by many consumers as a hostile and masculine environment, causing anxiety in customers, particularly at night. People were looking for a more friendly and even "domesticated" environment. For many years petrol station design had been neglected and forecourts were perceived by many as wastelands. Shell's competitors had already begun to make changes and sites were gradually evolving from garages which sell petrol to retail stores of the same quality as any other we might expect to find on the high street. If Shell was to retain market leadership, Shell too needed to review and update its image.

The consumer revolution of the 1980s firmly established powerful global brands - Shell had the opportunity to be in this league

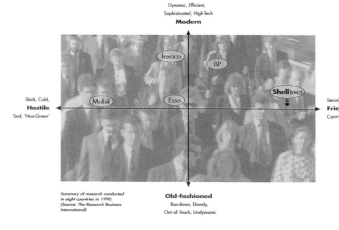

Shell's old identity (known as VM2) was friendly, but old fashioned

initial development sketches

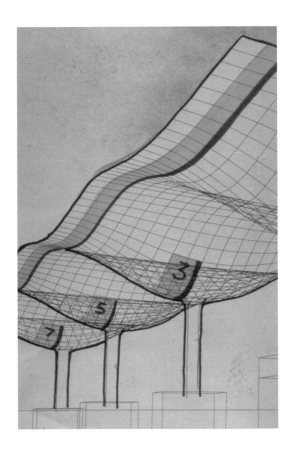

The RVI manual

small scale signage manufacture using craftsmen and labour - intensive sign installation in a developing country

mass production of signs and automated sign installation in a developed country

The existing design, known as VM2, dated from the 1970s. The name, logo and colours were recognised world-wide but they lacked a consistent application from country to country, leading to the appearance of multiple variations. With the increase in cross border traffic in some parts of the world, these differences had begun to cause brand confusion. If Shell was to retain its market position, this problem needed to be addressed in order to produce a consistent brand image. A visual manifestation of the Shell brand, which was globally consistent, would effectively convey a common message. VM2 was too limited in scope for this task, not helped by the fact that specifications were not detailed enough - they were only laid down in two-dimensional drawings with few construction or materials standards. This had led to individual interpretations as companies adapted VM2 to meet their own circumstances and conditions.

The outdated VM2 signage being removed

An early RVI site in Brazil

An RVI site in Canada

An RVI prime sign in Hong Kong featuring multiple sub brands

In 1990 Shell was the world's largest retailer in any category with 38,000 branded outlets outside the US, compared with Macdonald's 14,000 world-wide. As such Shell had a considerable influence on the retail trade as a whole. Brand image is always important but particularly given the competitiveness of the market. In a market where the products are very similar, design can tip the balance. Shell needed a design which travelled well and was instantly recognisable. The design also needed to be such that it could be retrofitted on existing stations as well as new sites. The Shell RVI was not just a cosmetic new look, but a carefully considered redesign driven by extensively researched consumer need analyses.

The new Shell RVI stations were designed to meet the same modern retail standards which people have come to expect from the high street. The design follows a generic industrial format in terms of materials, shapes and the practical presentation of the environment. Simple shapes and forms, together with a clear application of colour, succinctly communicate Shell's message and help to counterbalance the scale of sites and the busy, noisy environment. Great emphasis was laid on Shell's core strengths so that whilst modernising the sites, the inherent warmth of the Shell brand has not been lost.

Corner detail

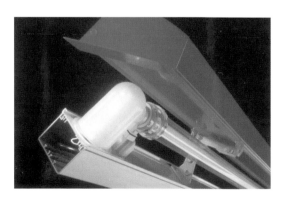

The Shell emblem or "pecten" was first used in 1904. Since then it has been changed a number of times, the last version dating from 1971. Its designer, the renowned Raymond Loewy, wanted it to be presented on a white background for optimum impact, but this was lost in the VM2 retail design. The RVI version is curved and three-dimensional for added vitality. All aspects of the new RVI design follow through from the pecten, in terms of its shape, its colours and its essence. The red/yellow colour balance is used throughout the RVI design system.

The organic curve of the pecten is echoed in the curves of the monolith, key signs and in particular on the canopy edge. These curves minimise the masculine preconceptions of the petrol forecourt and are intrinsically appealing in themselves.

The canopy fascia has a distinctive and innovative shape unique to Shell. It curves gently, and appropriately in the form of an 'S'. This softening of the appearance meets customers' demands for a more comfortable, friendly environment.

Detail of corner, a difficult problem to solve

Corner detail with lettering

"Slap-on" new image, applied to the existing old structure

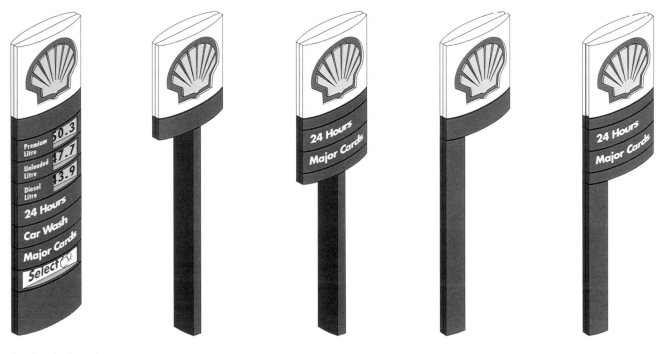

Family of prime signs

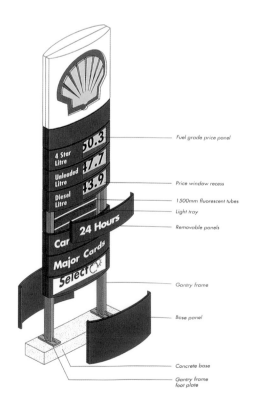

Fuel grade price panel

Price window recess

1500mm fluorescent tubes

Light tray

Removable panels

Gantry frame

Base panel

Concrete base

Gantry frame
foot plate

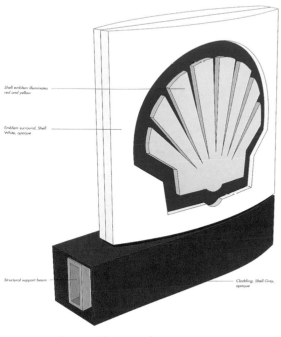

Shell emblem illuminates
red and yellow

Emblem surround, Shell
White, opaque

Structural support beam

Cladding, Shell Grey,
opaque

Construction sample

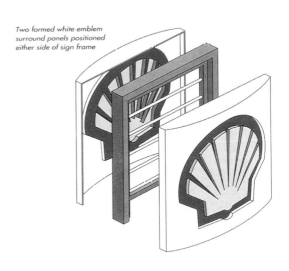

Two formed white emblem
surround panels positioned
either side of sign frame

The prime sign is the principal element of brand
display and is designed to be an efficient means
of communicating important site information. It
is a very effective, functional yet minimal design.
It is available in a wide range of variants, all of
which use common elements. This achieves
consistency in appearance as well as minimising
manufacturing costs.

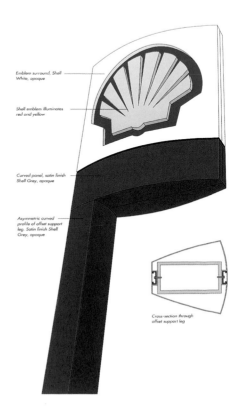

Emblem surround, Shell
White, opaque

Shell emblem illuminates
red and yellow

Curved panel, satin finish
Shell Grey, opaque

Asymmetric curved
profile of offset support
leg. Satin finish Shell
Grey, opaque

Cross-section through
offset support leg

"Flag" pole sign

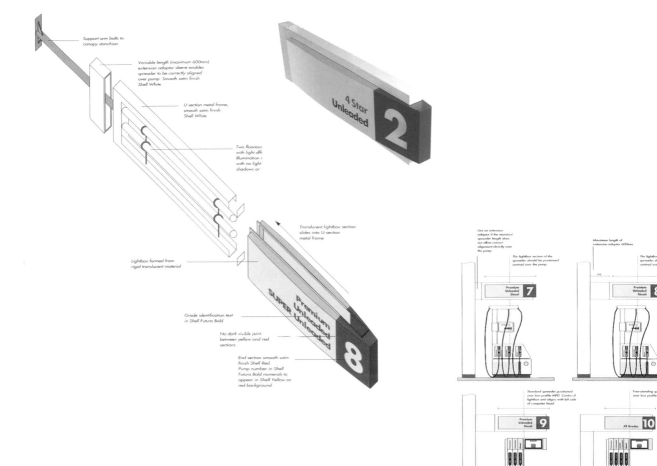

The colour balance is crucial. The primary colours of red and yellow are a strong branding tool and in combination are unique to Shell in this sector. Red and yellow are very powerful, particularly together. However, the colours used in the old design (VM2) were harsh and industrial. The new red and yellow are more warm and friendly. The extensive use of white enhances and offsets the red and yellow and helps to provide a clean, consumer friendly environment. The secondary colour grey, which harmonises with the yellow, red and white, contributes to the colour balance and is very good for surfaces prone to wear and tear. The colours are also used to identify services on site. Red with yellow is used for shopping and signage. Grey with yellow denotes car services and blue with yellow the carwash.

David Davis inspecting signage

Night view - light testing

Where previously petrol stations had been designed for the car, Shell's new forecourt format has been designed with its customers in mind. Making people feel welcome is at the heart of the new design. Good lighting is essential, to ensure the safety of the site but it can also be used as a powerful design tool. Too much harsh light is unwelcoming and too little leads to insecurity. Lighting should be inviting and make people feel relaxed. The new lighting minimises shadows and glare, but its spread is even, warm and inviting. The canopy lighting has been approached in a new way. Light is reflected onto it from behind the offset red bar, which gives a soft yet bright appearance. All the signs are prominently illuminated and the monolith is lit in such a way that the pecten appears to float which gives it a very distinctive quality, easy to spot from a distance.

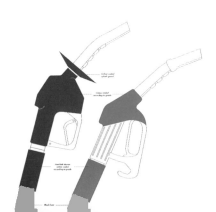

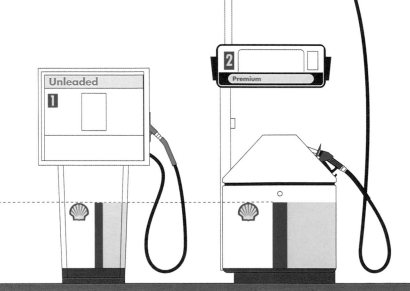

Graphics on pumps

Good graphics are also essential. The use of one main typeface, Shell Futura Bold, adds consistency and harmony to the design. It is modern, simple and crucially, highly legible.

The "logotype" is a specially designed typeface primarily used for brand name identification on the canopy. It replaced a previous logotype design which research showed to be old fashioned and rather "technical" rather than "retail". The new logotype is curved and three-dimensional on the canopy whereas the old design was flat and angular.

The most important new architectural feature of the new format is the portico, a simple white framing structure which supports the promotion of allied retail brands. It is a clever means of integrating and harmonising the other offers on site, enabling each forecourt to fulfil a number of diverse functions whilst retaining its essential identity.

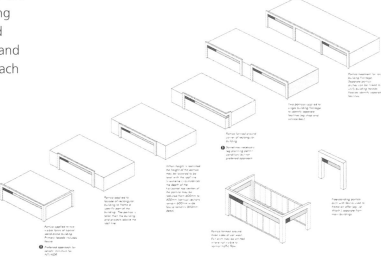

Modular system for building/shop

The choice and quality of materials used has also been essential to the success of the project. Those chosen are highly durable, represent value for money and are easy to maintain.

Shell has always spearheaded sensitive and contemporary design, applying the best principles of modern architecture. More so than in most buildings, a petrol station is determined by its function and an extreme logic lies behind Shell's forecourt designs. The new stations are authentic, and fulfil their task with discretion. They have a long history of associating with modern design. This powerful new visual interpretation has consolidated Shell's position of brand leadership and has enhanced its professionalism.

Addison, London has ceased to exist as a company specialising in the energy sector. David Davis, formerly senior designer at Addison for the Shell project, has now joined Minale Tattersfield Design Strategy.

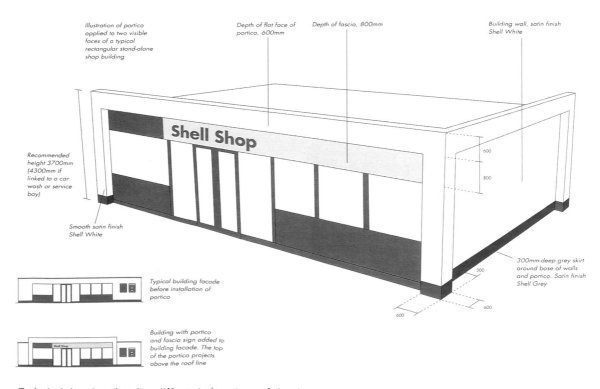

Illustration of portico applied to two visible faces of a typical rectangular stand-alone shop building

Depth of flat face of portico, 600mm

Depth of fascia, 800mm

Building wall, satin finish Shell White

Recommended height 3700mm (4300mm if linked to a car wash or service bay)

Smooth satin finish Shell White

Typical building facade before installation of portico

Building with portico and fascia sign added to building facade. The top of the portico projects above the roof line

300mm-deep grey skirt around base of walls and portico. Satin finish Shell Grey

Technical drawing showing different elevations of the shop

Shell's retail outlet - Select

Illuminated fascia for Select

Detail of the Select fascia

Full view showing the complete "landscape" of the Shell forecourt

Marcello Minale's comment

On the strength of the success of BP's updated forecourt design, Shell decided to tackle their network. With over 40,000 outlets world-wide, the design implementation was on a much larger scale. I give full credit to the management for their vision in taking this step and the organisation and speed with which the new design was implemented.

The independent red strip has proved a milestone in the evolution of the all-important canopy fascia. However, the components require a level of engineering more akin to the automotive industry, as opposed to what one might expect from the sign manufacturing industry. In my view, in certain markets the high standards necessary have not been achieved. The colour coding, however, has been well resolved and very consistently applied.

Shell was one of the first companies to champion the C-Store and its aim to make a living as a supermarket as opposed to a petrol retailer. They have made a brave attempt and the Select C-store brand has been well developed.

There is no doubt that both Shell and BP have become a point of reference for all other companies wanting to upgrade their networks.

04

brand identity and forecourt design by Wolff Olins
latest forecourt design by Foster & Partners

REPSOL

brand identity and forecourt design by Wolff Olins
latest forecourt design by Foster & Partners

With the longest name and shortest history the Instituto Nacional de Hidrocarburos (INH) was set up in 1981 to bring together the Spanish public companies operating the oil and gas industry. It had a decade to prepare for the opening up of Spain following its entry into the EEC, and the assault of Esso and Shell on the last plum market in western Europe.

By 1986, when Wolff Olins became involved, INH was known to only 2% of Spaniards who thought it was some kind of scientific bureau. Its companies had been streamlined into four groups: Hispanoil for exploration and production, EMP for refining and distribution, Alcudia for petrochemicals, and Enagas and Butano in natural and liquefied petroleum gas distribution. But INH was still much less than the sum of its parts. Spain's largest company and its first multinational was overshadowed by member companies with established traditions, stronger names and a place in their own right among Spain's top ten.

Before - the old identity

Identity by Wolff Olins

Repsol identity applied to racing car

The original sun logotype on fascia by Wolff Olins

But INH had found a more competitive name for the future. Then used on one of its lubricant brands, it was easy to pronounce and had established associations with energy. That name was Repsol. Wolff Olins was chosen to apply the name and a simple geometric sun logotype (designed by Landor) to its chain of a thousand petrol stations.

However, the possibilities of Repsol were to be pushed further. Wolff Olins argued that to limit the Repsol name to the group and petrol retailing did not make sense, any more than it would for Shell to have a different name for each of its activities. INH accepted the logic. It decided to pursue a single idea and reputation, and call everything Repsol. Wolff Olins advised that more ambitious imagery would convey a more confident company, a leader in the new Spain. To fulfil this role it should be modern but not modernist, striking but not outrageous, international but still Spanish. Less Euclid, more Miró.

Repsol's forecourt retail outlet - Repshop

Large city station by night

Small regional station by day

The new identity was vital to INH's transition from a state holding company to a vertically integrated energy group in the private sector. Commenting on the Repsol sun, Fernandez-Cuesta, Repsol's Director of Marketing says: "It is the first thing we have in common", relevant both internally and externally. "Here in Spain people see identity as a political issue, not as a necessity of the market. They don't realise how important corporate identity is for sales."

A pole sign

Fernandez-Cuesta commented: "We were living in unique years in the economic history of Spain. Between 1986 and 1992 we had to convert the oil monopoly to a normal free market situation. We had to change the entrepreneurial structures in all our companies. Yet even the process of adopting a new name and merging into a new group was very difficult." Corporate glue was needed as never before. Could the new identity provide it? Fernandez-Cuesta was optimistic. He remembers the moment when the identity emerged: "My first impression was, the spirit has changed."

Some aspects of the Repsol concept were controversial at first. Colour coding indicates which pumps dispense which product, on both spandrels and columns legible at 100 metres. "We were against this", says Fernandez-Cuesta, "as introducing too much colour under the canopy. But when we saw the service station prototype, we understood that it could work very well."

The columns are in fact ellipses - fat one way, slim the other - light in construction but offering a large surface for signage. Throughout, Wolff Olins took the normal architectural elements and gave them unusual forms. Along with the distinctive uplighting of the pump islands, this gave the stations an identifiable Repsol character, less brash than the average service station. The Repsol colour scheme also found a less emphatic way to use primary colours, with dark grey as the main canopy colour.

The two-year implementation programme covered everything from oil exploration teams in Gabon to the Butano trucks buzzing around Madrid; a thousand vehicles, stationery, forms, ships, packaging, signs, publications, uniforms, exhibitions, Butano shops and car oil-change centres.

Deputy marketing director Pedro Moraleda commented: "Our main task in the coming years is to change a Spanish company into a European company, and with this identity we can develop throughout Europe."

Moraleda was appreciative of the depth of detail in the design: the 26 background colours in eight colour groups which provide a palette for every need; the comprehensiveness of the manual: "Once you start to work with it, you find there is a solution for everything." And the typographic form of the Repsol name: "That S is one of the Wolff Olins team's great discoveries. It is in itself a piece of identity for Repsol."

Repsol Butano tankers

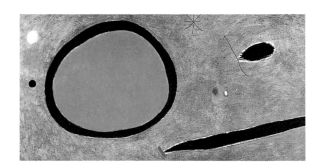

Spain and the inspiration of its art. The sun represents a new Spain in the international arena

Uniforms

REPSOL

Updated identity by Cruz Novillo

Above & below: updated versions by Addison España

upper tier version for prestigious sites

Norman Foster sketch, November 1996 (Foster & Partners)

In the years since 1992 Repsol has continued to be the main oil company in Spain despite the presence of global leaders in the industry. Its name, look and service standards gave it a pivotal role in Spain's emergence into renewed economic growth and dynamism. Spanish people and Spanish business are proud of Repsol and what it says about the potential of their country to match and outperform the best in the world.

With showers for truck drivers, free telephones, Repshops with vending and ice-making machines, bars and restaurants, Repsol offered a level of service and professionalism that Spain had never seen. Its aim was not to equal but outperform its international rivals when they began to compete in earnest.

But the story does not end here. Since the implementation of Wolff Olins designs in the 1980s, the market has continued to evolve. Motivated by an increasingly competitive global market and perhaps in response to the frequent criticism laid on petrol stations, that of being one of the most neglected structures on the modern landscape, Repsol is one of the only companies to have brought in an architect to reconsider filling station design from first principles. Foster & Partners has come up with a design which goes against the current trend of station design as inherently two-dimensional and signage based.

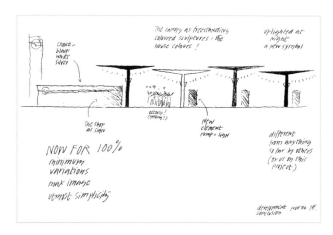

Norman Foster sketch, November 1996 (Foster & Partners)

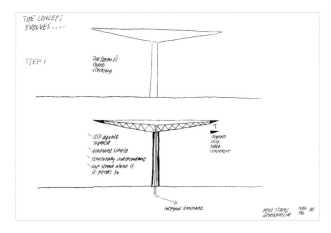

Norman Foster sketch, November 1996 (Foster & Partners)

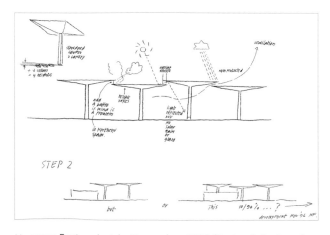

Norman Foster sketch, November 1996 (Foster & Partners)

View of canopies (Photographer: Nigel Young for Foster & Partners)

The new design boldly embraces three dimensions and centres on a new modular canopy system. The canopies are coloured in Repsol's corporate colours found within their logo. Their strong sculptural form and vibrant nature make them unique. Canopies provide shelter to the other systems. The shop unit, carwash, petrol pumps and signage elements belong to a related family of pure box-like forms.

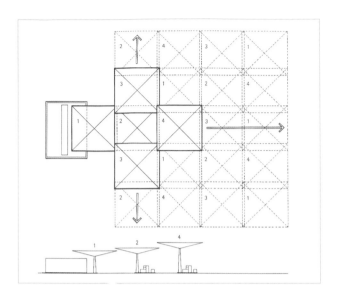

Overlapping canopy roof plan, indicating planning flexibility
(Foster & Partners)

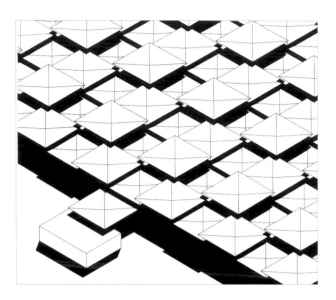

Overlapping canopy, isometric view indicating planning,
flexibility and expansion (Foster & Partners)

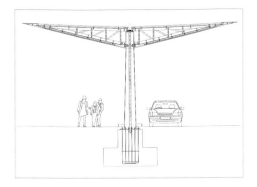

Modular canopy section indicating integral structure, cladding and roof drainage (Foster & Partners)

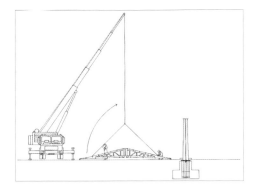

Modular canopy delivery on site (Foster & Partners)

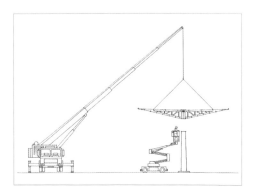

Modular canopy assembly on site (Foster & Partners)

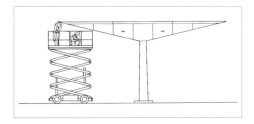

Modular canopy cladding and final commissioning on site (Foster & Partners)

The canopy is constructed with a lightweight steel space frame structure and composite aluminium skin. Each canopy deliberately overlaps its neighbour. So while several oil companies have had difficulty creating a truly universal and flexible modular system for the canopy, this solution with its variable overlapping feature provides flexibility in planning and accommodates the numerous variations of shop unit, pump island and site configuration.

Canopies and other elements are factory-made, transported to site and quickly installed, providing cost benefits while maintaining high quality standards and rapid delivery. The design enjoyed considerable acclaim at Lisbon's Expo '98 and two of these stations have opened in Barcelona and Madrid and are now being reproduced at 200 sites across Spain.

Final forecourt design: Repsol service station at night (Photographer: Nigel Young for Foster & Partners)

Marcello Minale's comment

The Repsol corporate identity updated by Wolff Olins, which portrays the Spanish sun à la Miró, is an excellent interpretation of the Spanish spirit and embodies the aspirations of corporate identity. It has also been very cleverly adapted for application to the canopy fascia and the result is unique.

More recently, Foster & Partners has produced a very striking sculptural design for Repsol. However, as I mentioned in my introduction, the new umbrella-style design works well on completely new sites but it is impossible to retrofit to an existing station.

05

preliminary concept by Minale Tattersfield & Acton
final design by Minale Tattersfield Design Strategy

ITALIANA PETROLI
preliminary concept by Minale Tattersfield & Acton
final design by Minale Tattersfield Design Strategy

Collaboration between Italiana Petroli (Italy's second biggest petrol retailer) and Minale Tattersfield & Acton first began in December 1995. It followed a decision by IP to update the image of its station network in order to compete with other major international oil companies. A crucial factor was that the design programme should be cost effective and that the new image could be applied to their existing 4,200 petrol stations. These restrictions meant that the new designs would be more an evolution of the existing identity as opposed to a complete revolution.

The new image is simple but suggests modernity, quality, technology and also represents value for money. Three principal elements, all interlinked, have been altered to bring about this new image: the totem, the fascia of the canopy and surrounding buildings and the sign system.

Previous forecourt design

Experimenting with logo shape

developments of the forecourt design

The first of the explorative proposals

Model of station layout

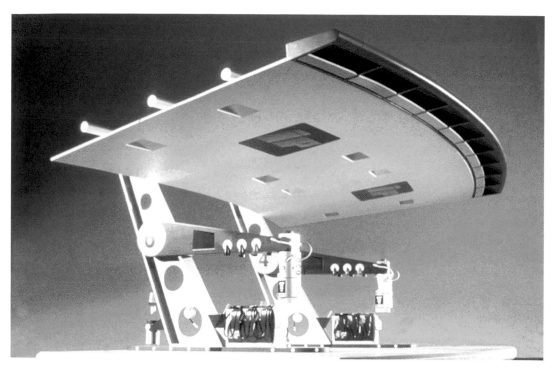

Preliminary proposal for a futuristic structure

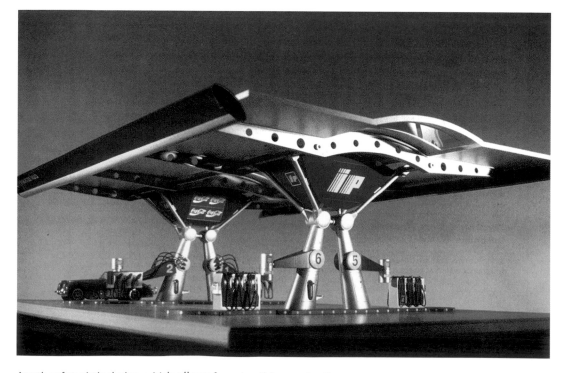

Another futuristic design which allows for advertising under the canopy

A "Sole-shaped" canopy design with double columns

A suspended video and monitor with pump on the ground

proposal for the restaurant and self-service area

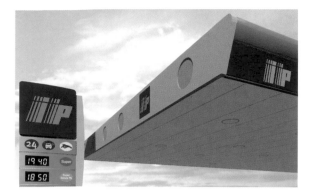

Detail of the "cheese wedge" canopy

Pictograms for sign system

The final station - the first of 1500

Bar and internet area

Proposal for final design

Bar area

Detail of fascia

Detail of bar

Detail of cladded columns

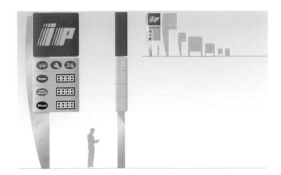

Modular totem system

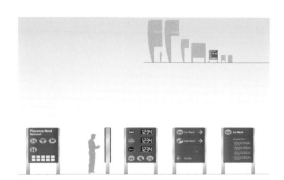

Modular self-standing system

Research was carried out into the different shapes and materials to be used for the totem. Prototypes were made and tested and finally a sail-shaped design with a body made from lightweight GRP and acrylic and a steel subframe was chosen. A modular system, it is economical and easy to manufacture. The IP colours of blue and yellow have been retained but brightened for greater impact. Metallic silver has also been added for a premium appeal.

Final sail-shaped version

Testing for visibility at night

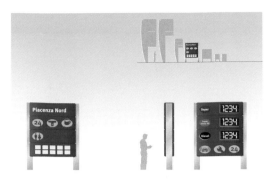

Modular self-standing system

Another proposal for totem

The totems are constructed in two sizes, either
7 metres or 3.90 metres depending on the
positioning and they can be used either with
or without the application of prices and services
available. Petrol pricing information is operated
electronically working on a seven-segment system
and can be changed both from the central
pay-point or from the base of the totem.

Detail of sign system

The first prototype

To update the fascia for greater impact an illuminated concave shell-like structure is applied to the existing canopy. This, like the totem, is a modular system manufactured from GRP in two-metre modules. This is both a cost effective and low maintenance option but achieves maximum impact. As no uniform canopy size had previously been used across the network, the new fascia is also easily adapted to these variations in size. Using the newly brightened IP colours of blue and yellow the fascia is illuminated from the yellow curved lip. The light also shines down on the blue cladding below where service information is applied. The effect created at night is a warm glow from the yellow shell whilst the service information is illuminated and clearly visible. The shell lip prevents dust from entering and enables the neon strip lights to be changed easily.

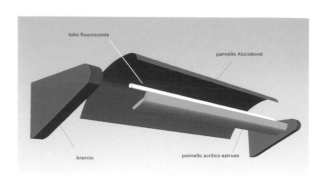

Exploded view of first canopy fascia prototype

Final prototype ready for testing

Corner detail of fascia

Building fascia side cladding

This cladding is applied to the sides of the building facing the driver as he enters whilst along the less prominent side, parallel to the road, a simple silver cladding with circle details is applied to reduce cost. The IP logo can also be applied in these circles.

The sign system to be applied to the fascia and totem was also in need of updating. Minale Tattersfield suggested a more modern and dynamic typeface and created over 30 new original pictograms to accompany it. A new, stand alone information board was also suggested to range in height from 1 metre to 3 metres, also in GRP and again using the brightened IP colours.

Around the same time it was decided to update the IP identity, the decision was taken to launch self-service pumps as an additional service across the network. To have both serviced and self-service pumps in operation on a single forecourt could potentially cause confusion so an identity was needed to demarcate clearly where each system was in operation. This led to the introduction of "Fai da te", an identity designed by Minale Tattersfield. It comprises a dark blue logo on a pale blue background reading "do it yourself" in Italian and a hand mimicking the action of filling a vehicle with petrol. It also clearly points to the pump. To draw further attention to the pumps where self-service is in operation, the structure column of the canopy is clad in vibrant pale blue and white stripes.

Striped column to signal self-service pumps

"Fai da te" on pump nozzles

Forecourt with IP Planet information kiosks

Solar panel sign signalling IP Planet station

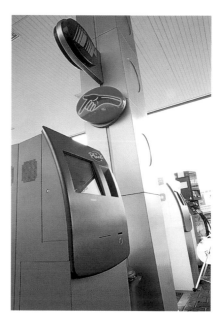

External information kiosk

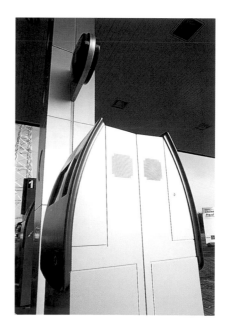

Side view showing two kiosks back to back

Internal information kiosk

IP continues to test new concepts in order to stay abreast of market changes and technological advances. These include concepts developed by Minale Tattersfield for a new service which potentially will be offered across the network. This service, known as "IP Planet", will provide an in-store banking service, parcel post, video rental, lottery and touch-screen information point. The concept was launched at the Bologna motor fair using digital video to present the "IP Planet" experience and is now on trial in seven of IP's principal service stations.

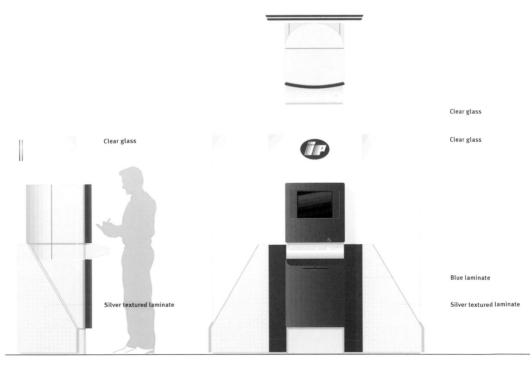

Concept drawing for internal information kiosk

Technical illustration: totem

Technical illustration: canopy

Screen shots from walk-through video for IP by Minale Tattersfield

The same detail of the canopy is applied to the shop fascia

Marcello Minale's comment

In terms of cost, durability and ease of maintenance the IP fascia has been a great success. The shell-shaped structure is energy-efficient with a single light source illuminating both the blue and yellow areas. It is also very easy to maintain. The totem is striking and unique. It is the optimum solution for a large network of over 2500 stations.

The fact that IP is willing to take on board new technology will ensure they keep up with the competition. They have already made good use of solar panels and with IP Planet they are heading towards the e-commerce station.

06

brand identity by Anisdahl, Sand & Partnere
station design by Odd Thorsen Design & Arkitektur

HYDRO TEXACO
brand identity by Anisdahl, Sand & Partnere
station design by Odd Thorsen Design & Arkitektur

In 1995 American oil company Texaco merged with Norwegian chemical company Norsk Hydro to form Hydro Texaco. Whilst the newly merged company clearly needed to rebrand, the merger also provided a good opportunity to develop a new station concept to complement the brand philosophy.

The Hydro Texaco merger coincided with a period of widespread public debate in Norway regarding the subject of forecourt architecture. Public opinion was against the increasing number of commercial developments being built which had nothing to do with Norwegian building culture. These were considered by many as scars on the Norwegian landscape. Large corporations were paying little regard to local customs or environmental concerns and were doing nothing to preserve the Scandinavian building traditions and materials. International oil companies were considered the major offenders. Pressure was put on the government to curb the visual aggression of these oil giants and in response the Minister for Cultural Affairs recommended new siting and design guidelines. Until this point, the term "Scandinavian design" had never been set out as a guideline for developing petrol stations in Scandinavia.

The new identity

Variation of brand identity

Hydro Texaco, and in particular design manager John Sandnes, wanted the new station design to adhere to these guidelines. The aim of the project was to develop a holistic visual profile with new aesthetic qualities and the new brand identity and station design were to work together to this end. The designs should be modern, simple and functional, appropriate to Scandinavian tastes and landscape and should project a friendly and personal image in direct contrast to what was considered the vulgarity of the oil giants. Anisdahl, Sand & Partnere was appointed to develop the new brand identity and Odd Thorsen Design & Arkitektur to create the station concept.

Research revealed that the names of both companies were equally well perceived in Scandinavia and so it was essential that both companies should appear as equal partners in the new identity. "However," remarks Leif Frimann Anisdahl, who together with his wife Kari was responsible for the brand design, "we decided from the outset that the two logos (the Texas star and Hydro's viking ship) should not be combined. The newly merged Hydro Texaco would start out with a completely new identity." The merger of the two companies is highlighted by the combination of the two letters, Y and X. This laid the foundations for the new brand identity and the solution is highly flexible. The X and Y when extracted can be used as an emblem in its own right, suited to numerous applications, and it quickly gained recognition amongst the Norwegian public.

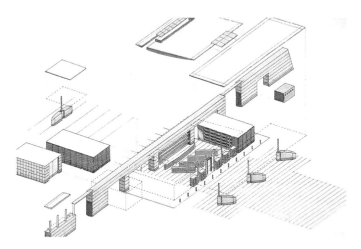

Technical drawing of site showing two sides of technical wall

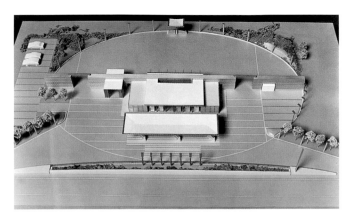

Aerial view of site

Odd Thorsen, who led the industrial design team, has for many years been responsible for the large majority of high profile public environmental projects in Norway. He made his name from his pioneering designs for the Norwegian National Railways (NSB), the largest public organisation in Norway. This meant that other large corporations soon followed suit. Other projects, such as the rationalisation of the Municipal Transport in Oslo and designs for the Olympic Games in Lillehammer, were quick to follow.

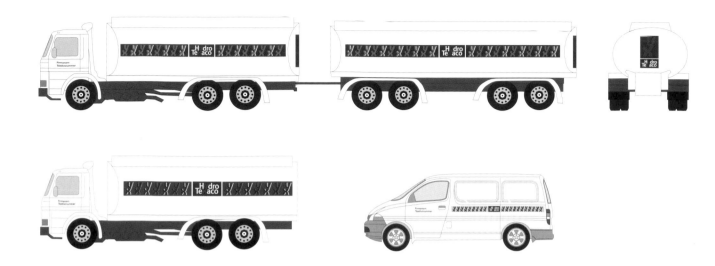

One of the key factors which influence Thorsen's work is his belief in the importance of semiotics and how this affects our environment, hence the influence this has on design. It is his belief that a structure should reflect its purpose by incorporating an understanding of the behaviour of the people that use it. This will ensure a functional design. Everything should have a scale of purpose and through design the environment should speak for itself. If a building reflects its function, then there will be no need for the visual vandalism caused by excessive signage. For example, a train station should look like a train station - and the optimum solution would be to make the trains visible to the users. In this way people would immediately understand their environment. Environments which are easy to understand have the advantage of being clean and harmonious in a structural sense, which helps to create the feeling of safety. Since architects are rarely trained in semiology, Thorsen has led the way in his field and his ideas have been highly influential on Scandinavian design.

Implementation of livery design

Uniforms

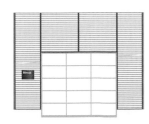

Front façade

Thorsen has also gained recognition as an advocate of the use of wood as a construction material for large-scale projects, both structurally and as cladding. As part of the early design team for the airport in Oslo he suggested wood beams should be used as structural supports in the terminal building and he has also used wood to build a number of large bridges.

Thorsen's philosophy appealed to Sandnes. As manager of the design programme he wanted the new Hydro Texaco station to be highly functional and self explanatory to its users. He wanted to avoid what he saw as the crazy competition amongst the large oil retailers to be the biggest and the brightest and he was reassured by Thorsen's careful consideration of the environment and materials. What Thorsen was suggesting was a clean and tidy environment without any circus. Visually it would be noiseless.

Drivers view of station approach

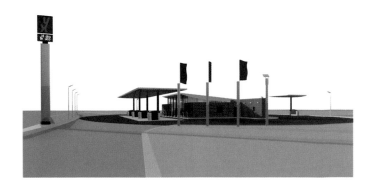

The design team (led by Thorsen and including Arild Eugen Johansen, Martin Krafft and Reiulf D. Ramstad) carefully constructed a visual profile of the new Hydro Texaco station, taking into account the complete range of factors which would influence the design. Subtlety was an important requirement - the building should identify itself as a petrol station without a brash application of branding. By establishing subtlety as its style it would be immediately recognisable as a Hydro Texaco station. Thorsen initially proposed a plain, oval-shaped aluminium column to identify Hydro Texaco sites. Pure and clean, this modern interpretation of an obelisk would stand as a landmark on the roadside and would require no branding. Ultimately, however, the client was not willing to take the risk since, in the competitive business of petrol retailing, optimum exposure is essential.

Site with unbranded roadside obelisk

Family of totems

Branded roadside column

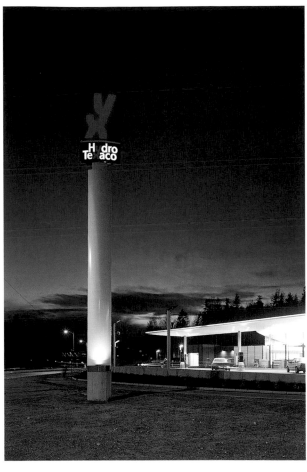

The new design had to be suited to three different types of site: new stations, existing station due to undergo extensive refurbishment and those for which the application of the new logo would suffice. There is also considerable variation in the size of sites: single pump stations with canopy usually located on industrial sites, small stations with a building and forecourt canopy, medium sized stations which might have a snack bar and C-Store and large sites with perhaps a self-service restaurant, car wash and servicing facilities.

Pricing element

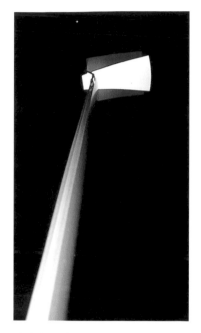

Lighting element

Perimeter lighting

A computer representation of the lighting system on site

The movement of traffic around the station was incorporated into the design from the outset. The sites are circular and the pivotal feature is a service wall which runs the length of the forecourt. This contains all the necessary services - water, electricity, drainage, compressed air, telephone lines, air ducts for extraction of fumes from the kitchen etc. Known as the technical wall, it is a plug-in system with operations on both sides. The front of the wall is the commercial side where the pumps are located and with access to the forecourt shop. The pump islands are angled to improve traffic flow. The diesel is located at the back of the technical wall together with car wash, air, vacuuming and other such facilities. This system allows for easy expansion as it is simple to extend the wall with minimum disruption to the site as pipes and cables do not have to be moved. Channels which collect residue oil and water lead from the forecourt to the technical wall where they are recycled, demonstrating practical yet environmental thinking. This marks a radical departure from typical petrol stations which are built like traditional buildings with the services scattered around the site.

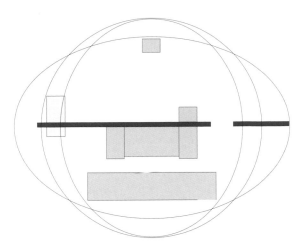

Traffic flow around the site with the technical wall as the pivotal point

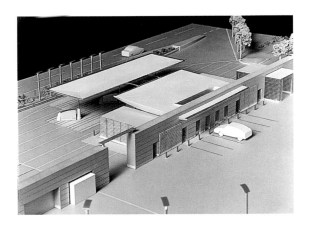

Technical side of service wall

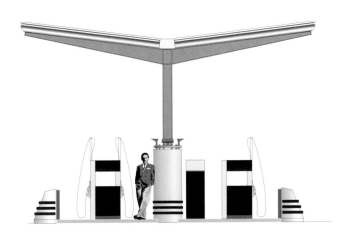

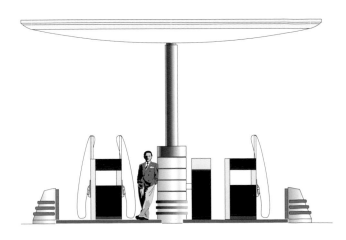

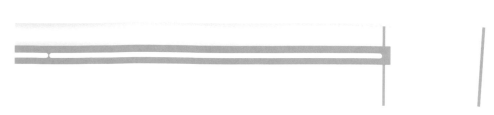

Detail of canopy on new stations

Detail of retrofit canopy

Station at night

The materials used to construct the station are distinct from those used by international retailers and are designed to give an organic appearance appropriate to the Scandinavian environment. They are not intended to be luxurious - more utilitarian for a natural look. The technical wall is clad in a slate-style material composed of fibrous cement. The forecourt shop and restaurant are glass fronted to give an open impression and the other service buildings are clad in 2″ x 2″ wooden slats stained an earth brown colour. The car wash is clad in corrugated metal. Uplighters create a warm light which is sufficiently bright but not brash. The wooden slats form a profile element. Built on a modular system, they are applied to a steel frame and can be used to reshape any existing building.

Glass fronted convenience store

Slim-edged station canopy

The forecourt has a simple, slim edged canopy with only a light strip at its edge for brand recognition. The aim is to create a balance between exposure through the use of graphic symbols and exposure through other elements. Since the Hydro Texaco brand is manifest in the complete environment, the corporate identity as a brand device can be used with subtlety on a roadside mast, flags around the site and for directional signage. Colour schemes have also been adopted for the different categories of station - yellow on all branded elements for Uno X (small sites with automatic payment units); larger Hydro Texaco sites are red and blue with a yellow undercanopy and diesel stations use red.

A prototype station has been built at Vinterbro outside Oslo and plans are in place to introduce the new design concept throughout Denmark and Norway.

The new Hydro Texaco station set within the landscape

Marcello Minale's comment

This station is very appropriate for the Scandinavian landscape and ecologically it is very sound. It could, however, prove expensive to reproduce the concept across a large network and be difficult to maintain on an international level. Nonetheless, it is a very interesting project and a stylish design!

07

designed by Minale Tattersfield & DASC

ELINOIL

designed by Minale Tattersfield & DASC

Independent Greek petrol retailer, Elinoil, is one of
Greece's only national retailers to operate on the
Greek Islands. With an existing network of 350
stations, Elinoil planned to buy a further 500
stations. In view of this expansion, the decision was
taken to rebrand the whole network. All the newly
acquired stations would of course have needed
rebranding anyway and many of the existing
stations looked tired and out-of-date.

Many of the large multi-national corporations such
as Shell, BP and Mobil already had a strong presence
in Greece operating as usual under their powerful,
but very international-style branding. Elinoil, on the
other hand, saw their key brand equity as their
excellent reputation amongst Greeks of being a
friendly and approachable service provider. Care
had always been taken to offer a service which
was tailored to local needs and it was never their
intention to roll out a vast corporate programme
which would destroy the character of the small
villages where many of the stations are located.

Old logotype

Before: Elinoil forecourt

Greek flag - the inspiration for the new logo!

New logotype - shortened to Elin (Greece), it portrays a sail at sea

Proposal for new logotype

Testing for readability

Minale Tattersfield, together with their Greek partners DASC, were appointed to create a new identity which would reflect the company's Greek origins and a station design which would be sensitive to the local environment. With DASC's inside knowledge of the region and understanding of Greek culture and Minale Tattersfield's extensive experience of designing for the energy sector, the partnership was ideally suited to Elinoil's needs.

Dolphin

Sea Eagle

Seagull

Wave

Wing

preliminary
proposals
for symbol
and totem

Development of family of totems

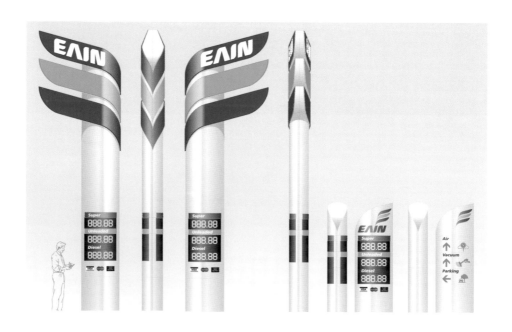

Preliminary development of station

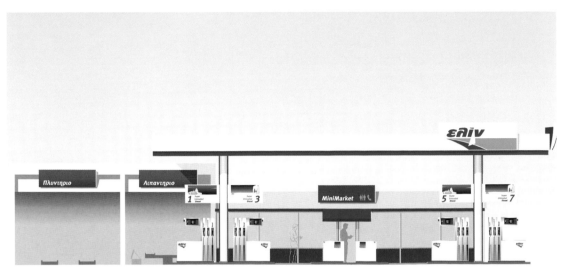

Preliminary development from front

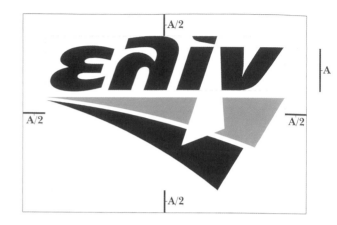

With this in mind, Minale Tattersfield & DASC came up with the design for a brand identity which focuses on the use of clean lines and colours which are particularly suited to the sunny Greek climate. They advised that the word 'oil' should be dropped from the logo and the name 'Elin', meaning Greek, should stand alone. This is represented in Greek characters. The two bands of blue from the old identity have been retained but brightened for a more modern and vibrant effect. The extensive use of white emphasises the clean, sweeping lines. These colours reflect the sea and sky and also the colours used in the island architecture. This animated design includes a white sail with the pennant at its top doubling as the accent of Elin. It represents a radical break from the yellows and reds traditionally associated with petrol stations.

Information icons

application of corporate identity

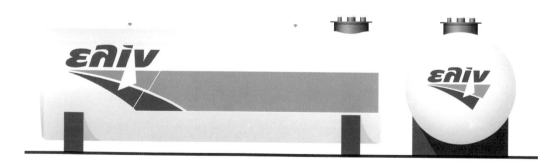

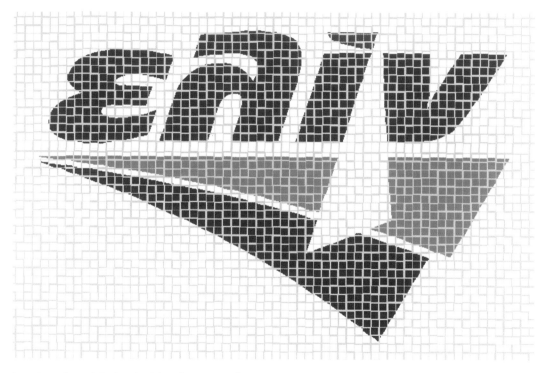

Logotype for printed material such as annual reports

Development of uniform design

When it came to the design of the station structure a further factor had to be taken into consideration. Unlike the multi-national retailers who tend to own all their sites, a large proportion of Elinoil's stations are franchised - garage owners who have chosen to buy into the Elinoil corporate image. It was very important that these owners should not be alienated by the new design. Equally it was important that the corporate look could be achieved with the minimum outlay. The Elinoil sites are hugely diverse - from a petrol pump on the street outside a row of shops, to large motorway filling stations with numerous pumps and additional services on offer. So the new system needed to be highly flexible.

The designs are created on a modular system which has the advantage of being easily applied to the existing station structure. A single logo panel can be applied to the canopy, whatever its size, providing complete versatility. In addition, new spreader panels above the pumps are designed to carry abstract images reflecting Greek culture.

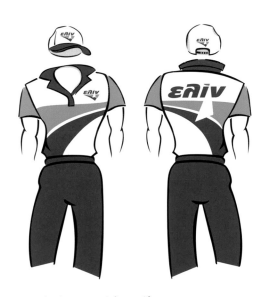

Final proposal for uniforms

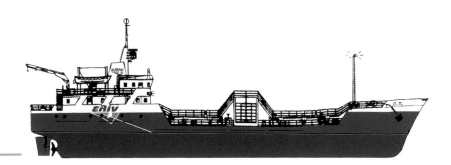

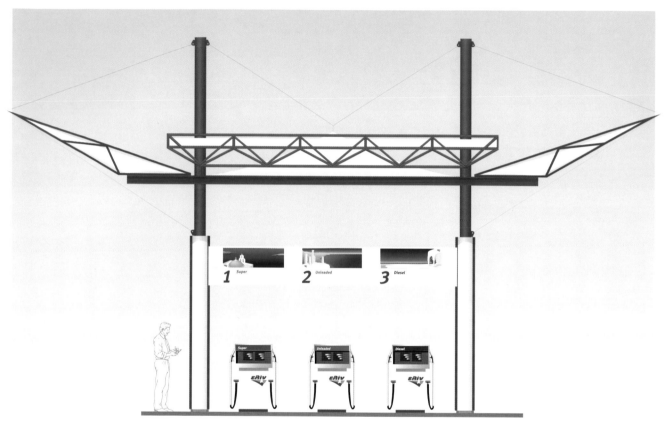

Special 'sail station' for Greek Islands, where space is very limited

A simple, modular system has been designed for
the principal roadside pole sign. Again, it provides
the necessary flexibility required by the large variety
of sites. A cost effective option, it can also be used
with or without prices. This low tech, modular pole
system forms the basis for the family of signage to
be used on larger sites.

Family of totems

Application on existing pole

24 Ωρες

Λιπαντήριο

Πετρελαιο Θερμανσης

Final design for totem

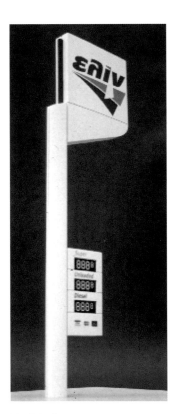

Model of totem

Final design to be applied to Elinoil's 350 stations

Marcello Minale's comment

Our designs for Elinoil were very minimal with the emphasis on the colours blue and white - Greece's national colours. The word 'oil' was quickly eliminated from the new logotype as unnecessary, particularly given today's increased interest in the protection of our environment. It was a challenge to produce a logo which could be read both in Greek letters and internationally but the sail solution proved very successful.

We experimented with a lot of different totem signs, but ultimately, being a retrofit system, the simple modular pole signs which are easy to apply worked the best. In fact, this family of signs in my opinion is one of our best. Long live Greece and their wonderful colours which inspired our solution! A special thanks goes to our partners DASC in Athens for their splendid contribution.

08

station design by Minale Tattersfield Design Strategy

LUKOIL
station design by Minale Tattersfield Design Strategy

With the fall of communism national Russian oil retailer, LUKoil, became subject to the same market forces as most other large retailers throughout the world. The effects became immediately apparent as major brands, in particular BP, moved aggressively into the Moscow area, fast on the heels of other global retailers such as McDonalds. LUKoil was quick to react. It was clear that they must embrace open market values in order to compete with these market giants and so appointed Minale Tattersfield Design Strategy to come up with a design for a new retail visual identity. No market research had been conducted which left the brief very open. In fact, Minale Tattersfield had little more to go on than that they should use their skill and expertise to come up with a suitable solution.

The first step was to examine the brand identity from both a consumer and corporate perspective. The existing logo was clearly very distinctive and LUKoil had specified that it should be kept. It also appeared to be quite well respected by both the business community and consumers, but it was important to identify the key brand equities in order to discard any negative elements. The protagonist brand colour was red and this was kept. Despite obvious connotations in a former communist country, its inherent dynamism and eye-catching effect outweighed any negative associations. However, the colour black also featured heavily, both as a black oil drop within the logo and in various applications on the existing station. David Davis, leading designer on the project explains: "This we strongly recommended them to drop since it focused too heavily on the negative connotations of oil and said nothing about LUKoil as a dynamic, modern retailer which puts its customers first."

Former 'black oil drop' identity

Two variations for final logo design

Existing symbol retained by designers

Existing identity on canopy

Whilst it was apparent that LUKoil was potentially interested in a radical solution, there were strong practical constraints which were going to limit the scope of the project. One of the primary concerns was that the canopy structure should be able to support the weight of up to ten feet of snow for six months of the year, as would be necessary in certain parts of Russia.

The colour white had been used extensively in the old station design, which meant they quickly took on a shabby appearance as any dirt was immediately visible. Also, when seen against a snowy landscape, the stations merge into the background reducing their impact on the passing motorist.

initial ideas & development for canopy design

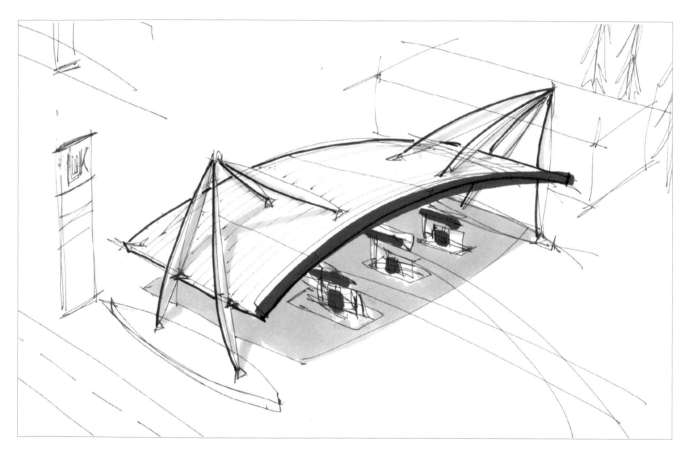

Arch 'tensile' style

Smooth bridge style

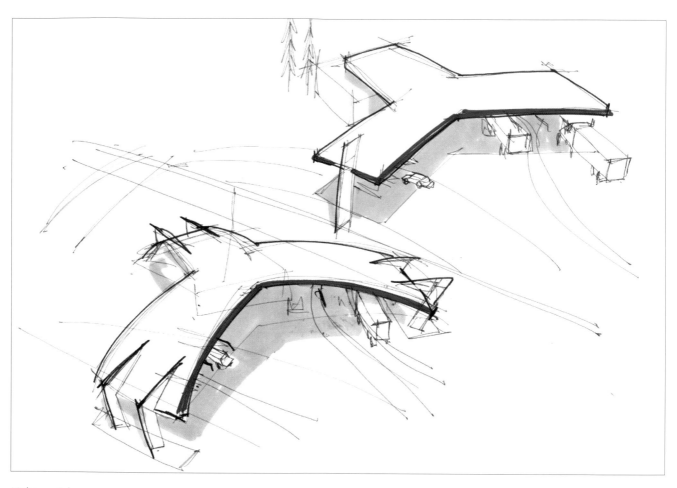

Y-shape style

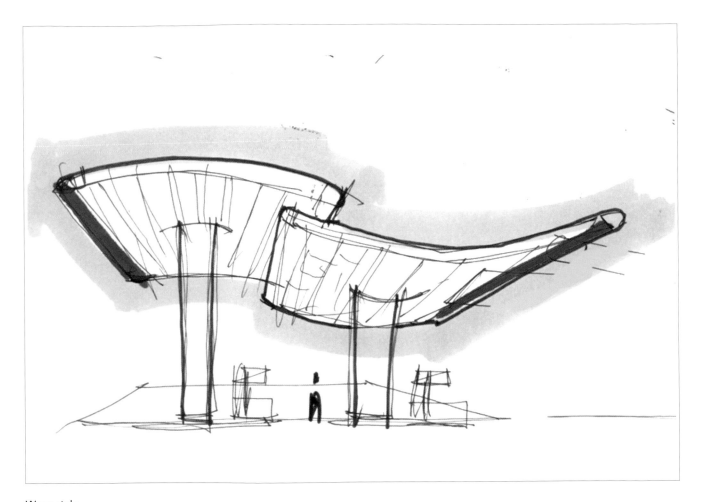

Wave style

Perspective view of proposed arched canopy design

Another key factor to be considered was the freezing temperatures which take hold in many parts of Russia for large proportions of the year. A design which offered protection from the elements (not only from snow and rain, but icy temperatures as low as -40°C, often accompanied by chilling winds) would offer considerable advantages over competitors. Minale Tattersfield came up with a number of variations on a dome-type structure to shelter the motorist from rain and snow and to offer protection against biting winds whipping around the sides, which can make filling the car an unpleasant task.

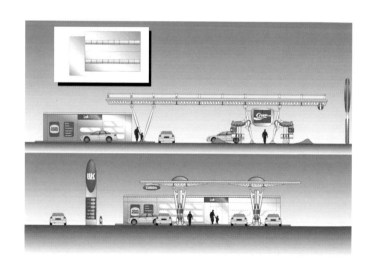

Proposal for elevated 'flying' petrol pumps

Elevation of arched canopy design

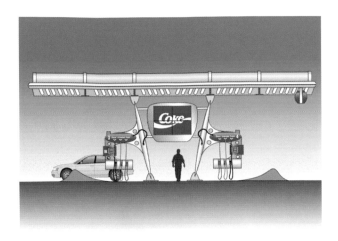

Close-up of 'flying' pump

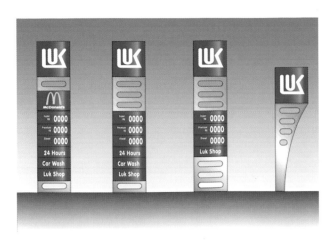

Proposal for family of totems

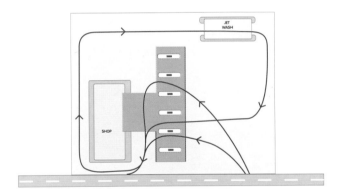

Petrol station plan and traffic flow (no.1)

Sign system

Another concept put forward by Minale Tattersfield was to maximise the available retail space by building upwards. A two-storey building could accommodate the forecourt shop and a partner brand such as Macdonalds, which has proved a great success in Russia. Another alternative would be to have a cyber café. Building upwards is particularly suited to urban areas where land is at a premium. Minale Tattersfield predicts that this will become a growing trend in future years, made necessary by a growing shortage of land in urban centres.

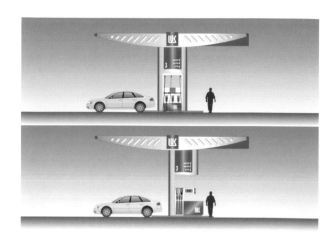

Petrol pump alternatives

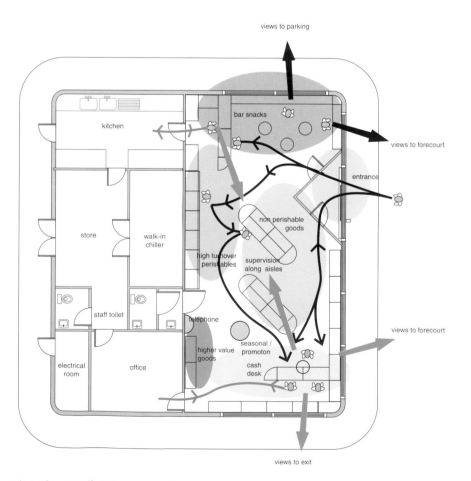

Plan of a LUKoil convenience store

various applications of "wing" station

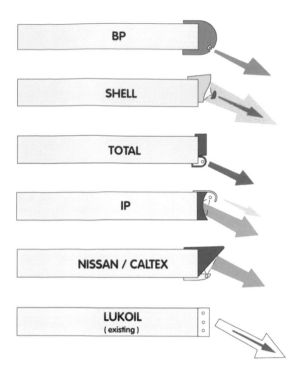

Research - looking at how competitors' fascias are lit

Direction and projection of lighting system

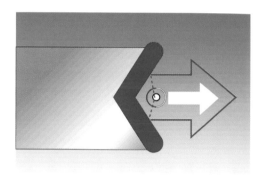

Detail of "K" canopy lighting system

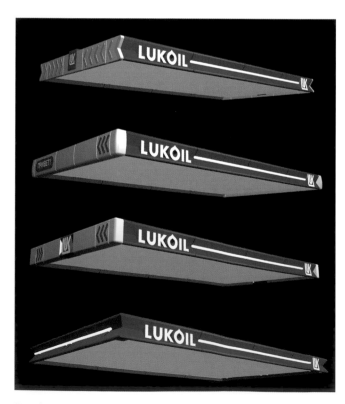

Development of "K" canopy design

Ultimately, as is often the case in these situations, LUKoil engineers felt more comfortable with a conventional station design where the principal means of differentiation lies in the branding of the station. The new design builds on the brand equities, using the colour red, the name and in particular the distinctive angle of the "K" of LUKoil, which has been worked into the uniquely shaped canopy edge. In addition, the unusual lozenge shape of the logo has been picked out in other branded elements such as signage. It has also been used in elements of the building. In cold environments full-height glazing can prove impractical and so a system was devised to incorporate a small, half lozenge shape into the windows. These help to reinforce the brand whilst avoiding the often austere and uninviting appearance of a building with small windows.

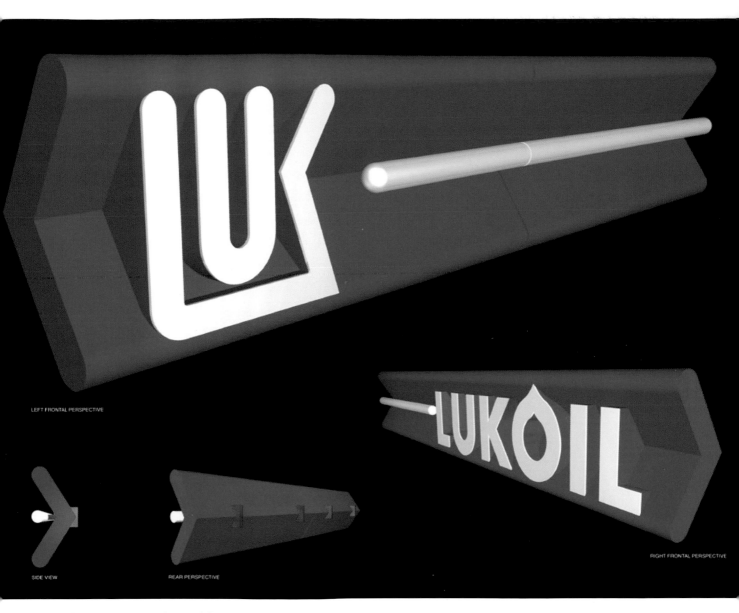

LEFT FRONTAL PERSPECTIVE

RIGHT FRONTAL PERSPECTIVE

SIDE VIEW

REAR PERSPECTIVE

Details of various aspects of LUKoil fascia design

View of "wing canopy" station at night

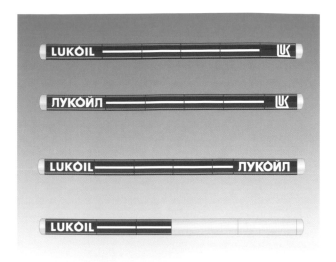

Front views of "K" fascia proposals

Side views of "K" fascia proposals

Suspended view of full "K" canopy detail

proposals for three petrol pump islands - changes in size and structure

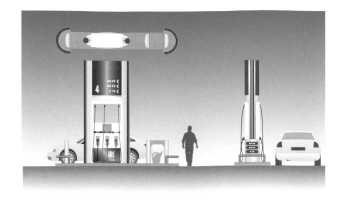

Previous experiments by LUKoil showed a high level of expertise in the production and application of cladding, which could provide a viable solution. Silver metal cladding panels have been used to avoid the extensive use of white, which quickly takes on a shabby appearance.

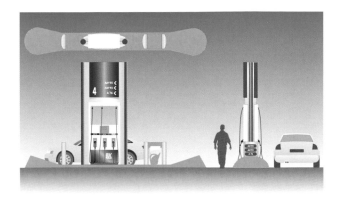

final proposals showing various views and details of site and station design featuring "K" canopy

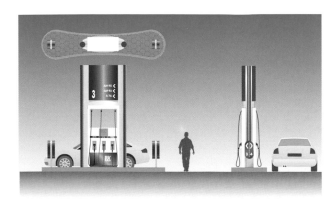

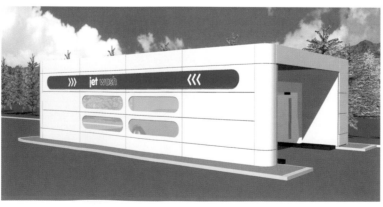

Station and combined tyre repair and jetwash centre

Close-up of combined tyre repair and jetwash centre

Adaptions to existing retrofit

Minale Tattersfield faced an unusual situation when it came to the design of the convenience store. Due to the slow and difficult transition from communism to a free market economy where supply problems and shortages continue, LUKoil thought a strongly branded C-store inappropriate. To promise too much would lead to disappointment and anyway, the idea of welcoming customers to a shop is unheard of in Russia. So the clearly differentiated brand of "Previt", (meaning "welcome" in Russian) was abandoned and the generic brand name of StarMart was chosen.

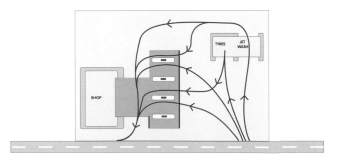

Petrol station plan and traffic flow (no. 2)

  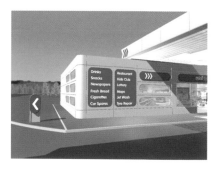

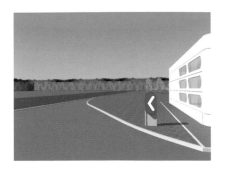 

Screen shots from walk-through video designed for LUKoil by Minale Tattersfield

Final proposal for approach view with distinctive "K" canopy

Marcello Minale's comment

Designing for LUKoil was an interesting exercise. Why? This was because in Russia the culture of international style petrol stations does not yet exist, despite the presence of one of the largest operators in the sector, LUKoil. It proved challenging to convince them that they did in fact need an international look to their station network.

We were also all surprised when they accepted the colour scheme of red and white.

In terms of design, the difficulty lay in creating a canopy which was unmistakably LUKoil. I think we achieved our goal. The unique shape of the canopy solves the problem successfully.

09

forecourt design by Euro RSCG Paris
implementation by Minale Tattersfield Piaton & Partners

YPF

forecourt design by Euro RSCG Paris
implementation by Minale Tattersfield Piaton & Partners

YPF was privatised in 1993, after which it developed from a state-owned megalith to a dynamic and competitive private market force. It is the largest Argentinian oil company, enjoying a 50% market share with a distribution network of around 3000 service stations. The company wanted designs for the petrol stations to reflect their new status.

The contract went to Euro RSCG, Paris. The design they created was highly innovative - a suspended structure, which for the first time left the forecourt free of any pillars, to give a clean and uncluttered appearance.

The contract to implement the new designs fell to Minale Tattersfield Piaton & Partners, the Latin American arm of Minale Tattersfield Design Strategy.

The most recent development in the YPF story is its acquisition by Spanish oil company, Repsol. Minale Tattersfield & Piaton has been appointed as design consultants to the newly merged company and the next challenge will be to integrate the two identities.

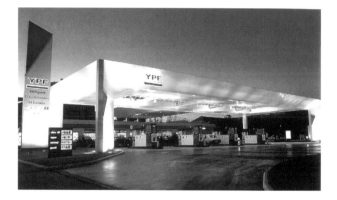

Design proposal for YPF petrol station

Marcello Minale's comment

The design is unique and it is considered by many to be the most innovative station ever built.

The new system was easy to introduce on completely new sites. However, it was rather more difficult to retrofit it to an existing site. Given that the original design was created in 1993 it has lasted very well.

10

name, brand identity and station
design by Wolf Olins

Q8

Kuwait Petroleum International was the first OPEC producer to develop its own downstream network, based on a retail network acquired from Gulf Oil. Following this acquisition, Wolff Olins was originally approached in 1985 and asked to develop KPI's new identity and station concept. As this had to compete with established oil giants like BP, Shell and Esso, it needed to be compellingly different and at the same time, visually appealing.

The initial project comprised three main components. The first was the creation of a brand identity which would quickly establish itself as a reputable international service brand, whilst also maintaining an indirect link with Kuwait. Secondly, this new retail network required a petrol station concept which would be more than just a place to refuel. In order to be considered a viable alternative to the major retailers which dominated the industry, the new Kuwait Petroleum petrol stations needed to represent a total environment, offering customers more control and choice through the retail experience. Finally it was necessary to develop an implementation programme covering all stations, initially in six European countries and subsequently world-wide.

The new symbol - designed by Wolff Olins

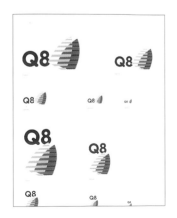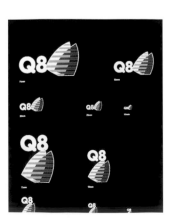

The symbol's adaptability and use on various backgrounds

Detail showing vibrant colours

After extensive research into possible new names, Wolff Olins put forward Q8 as the new brand name. A simple but effective device, it says Kuwait phonetically but does not look like Kuwait the country. Internationally the name is now pronounced in English like "7-Up".

Once the name had been established Wolff Olins developed a mark. Drawing on the Kuwaiti tradition of overseas trade, the new identity features a modern interpretation of a sail. The identity colours were chosen to be restrained and environmentally understated, with primaries used only for the brand mark. A typographic style was also developed for Q8, using a restricted number of typefaces which were instantly recognisable but less aggressive than had become common in the industry.

A major part of the branding programme for Q8 centred on the design and implementation of petrol stations. The scheme was devised to take account of the diversity of the European Gulf petrol station network which KPI had acquired. It had to be flexible enough to cover both flagship stations and road side filling points.

The station design reinforced the brand principles through the use of simple architectural forms and clear layouts. On major sites, pump hydraulics and electronics are encased in structural columns. The forecourts are lit like a supermarket while the canopy is unlit, except for the brand mark. This again made Q8 much less aggressive in appearance than its competitors, a fact which research showed pleased motorists.

The shop was seen as a major element in developing brand loyalty and the final design centred on interiors that were fully visible from the forecourt, highly accessible and welcoming.

Site with shop and high level pole sign

Detail of shop and pumps

Detail of pumps and shop

The first stage of the implementation was to apply the concept in six European countries, across 3000 petrol stations. This process had to be comprehensive, involving the support and involvement of many Q8 personnel, to ensure effective delivery.

An international steering group of national retail managers was set up by Wolff Olins to oversee the implementation. Briefing and design workshops ran by Wolff Olins helped to establish the concept along with the contribution of customer groups.

The new fascia with additional dynamic red stripe

A key concern of the implementation team was cost-effectiveness. Each region operated as a profit centre, so solutions had to meet local cost criteria without compromising quality standards. To ensure these were met, production prototypes were manufactured in six countries, feedback gathered and standards established. This set the benchmarks for choosing preferred suppliers.

Vehicle carrying lubricants

Finally Wolff Olins worked with Q8 engineers on technical and visual guidelines to ensure that quality was achieved consistently and in the most progressive way.

The branding programme proved a great success. Although Q8 was competing from scratch against some of the world's best known brands, such as Shell, BP and Esso, today Q8 is an established international petrol retailer, expanding fast into Eastern Europe and the Far East.

By 1992, more than seven years after the scheme was implemented, the Q8 brand needed refreshing. Wolff Olins was invited back to review the Q8 retail network and make recommendations for improvement. The resulting changes included a rationalisation of the brand mark and designs for the forecourt canopy and signage.

Most recent version of identity as applied to pole sign

Final design of the Q8 station

Marcello Minale's comment

Wolff Olins came up with a very valid branding
solution. However, in recent years the Q8 stations
have begun to look rather old fashioned and it is
now time for the identity to be refreshed.

11

brand identity and station design by
Minale Tattersfield & Acton

THAI OIL
brand identity & station design by Minale Tattersfield & Acton

Thai Oil has for a long time been a major player in the oil refining industry and through this activity it has achieved a very strong market presence in the energy sector. But it is only in more recent years that the decision was taken to expand into petrol retailing. In 1995 the company was floated which prompted an update to the brand identity, coupled with the need to develop a completely new retail identity and forecourt design for their proposed retail network in Thailand.

New identity

Previous identity and station design

New station set in a typical Thai tropical setting

Totem with two-horned logo derived from a rhino illustration

Historically oil companies have proved very weak retailers, often placing greater emphasis on their upstream activities such as exploration, extraction and refining. Retailing, of course, requires a different approach, particularly when the principal product being sold varies very little from one retailer to the next, which is the case with petrol and diesel. "This complacency has enabled other, more practised retailers, such as large supermarket chains, to encroach on what has traditionally been the preserve of the oil companies, vastly reducing their market share," comments a senior designer who worked on the project. "For this reason it was essential to have a brand identity which not only looked highly credible to potential investors, but one that could also be easily adapted to the retail network to project a customer friendly, retail character, whilst still clearly linked to the Thai Oil corporation."

Minale Tattersfield & Acton was awarded the contract to design Thai Oil's brand identity and to develop the new retail identity and forecourt design for their entry into the petrol retail market. Building on its existing position as a well respected, technologically advanced company, Thai Oil wanted its retail network to be positioned as a quality modern retailer of international stature.

Forecourt showing underside of canopy

For some time Thai Oil had been using an illustration of a rhinoceros, designed by the company chairman, as a promotional mascot. They were keen to maintain and build on this equity, however tenuous its connection to the oil industry might seem. Minale Tattersfield & Acton believed, however, that a very workable solution could be achieved, despite the fact that at first glance a rhinoceros appears to have little to do with the oil industry. By abstracting the rhino horns, Minale Tattersfield & Acton succeeded in capitalising on the power of the beast, with all its positive associations, to create a powerful and dynamic modern symbol, which also evokes the energy of the flame of the refinery.

the convenience store & cafe - Rhino Mart

Colours were selected with the sunny Thai climate and the Asian love of bright colours in mind. A cool mint combines with the vibrant magenta of the rhinoceros horns to achieve immediate impact. · Whilst to Western eyes this colour combination might at first appear garish, in its local environment it sits very comfortably. This theory is backed up by Q8's decision to brighten its corporate blue when used on station forecourts in sunny Asia.

One of Thai Oils competitors - showing the typical Thai style of bright colours and 'busy' environment

Identity applied to storage tank

Refinery entrance feature

Identity applied to tanker

Since it is rarely recommended to have a completely separate retail identity, small horns are used for corporate usage and larger ones for the retail environment, making it a highly flexible identity. As an abstract image it has a global appeal while in its use of vibrant colours it has captured a strong element of the East. In this way it appeals to the local market but travels very well abroad. In addition to creating this new brand identity and marque, Minale Tattersfield & Acton produced a comprehensive guideline manual to ensure consistent application throughout, from stationery to the livery for the Thai Oil fleet ships.

The new retail identity and filling station design was launched on 30th March 1995 with the opening of the flagship site on the Bagna Trad highway outside Bangkok. The design has clearly succeeded in its intention of appearing modern and high-tech, whilst maintaining a customer-friendly appearance which is polished and confident. The new design combines the corporate and retail image into a fully integrated 2D/3D solution, giving continuity and coherence to all of Thai Oil's operations and clearly positioning them as a modern, dynamic and international corporation.

Car wash graphics

Final forecourt design

Marcello Minale's comment

This project marked Thai Oil's entry into the downstream market so the stations could be designed from scratch. Hence, the design was not constrained by the need to develop a retrofit system. This provided the freedom to design the unique winged canopy which I think has proved very successful, particularly at night when the light spills out onto the underwing.

12

brand identity and station design by
Minale Tattersfield & Acton

PETRON

brand identity and station design by Minale Tattersfield & Acton

When Shell and Caltex entered the petrol retail market in the Philippines, Petron began to lose ground. Anxious not to forego their position as one of the market leaders, they quickly responded to the new competition. Consumer research suggested that Shell's image was perceived considerably more favourably than their own. Since their merger with Saudi Aramco, enough finance had become available to carry out an extensive reimaging project in order to revitalise the flagging brand which had merely evolved from the former Exxon identity.

The intention was to create a new corporate identity and a retail identity which was clearly linked to the former. Both would then be simultaneously relaunched with a large media spectacle in the hope of capitalising on the inevitable publicity. In this way it was hoped they would be able to leapfrog the competition.

New Petron logo

The old identity applied to totem and station

Minale Tattersfield & Acton was appointed as consultants to the project and began by determining Petron's existing brand equities. While the "P" of Petron was viewed quite favourably, the oil drop was too closely associated with its upstream activities. It did nothing to suggest a dynamic company which had embraced retail values. However, the concept of the oil drop was not entirely abandoned and instead it was incorporated into the new identity as an abstract expression of oil. This lead to the development of the fluid "P" which built on elements of the old identity but expressed them in a more modern, dynamic and customer-focused manner.

Canopy and petrol pumps with the fluid "P" styling

Petron wanted immediate differentiation from the other major players active in the Philippines (Shell and Caltex), and so whereas red had previously been the predominant brand colour, blue was introduced as the protagonist. An element of red was still retained, however, in a supporting yet significant role in order to retain a link with the old identity.

Since both the corporate and retail identity had to be redesigned, it left Minale Tattersfield & Acton complete flexibility to incorporate the two. Similarly to Thai Oil, the fluid "P" symbol is easily adapted to its retail application. It has the flexibility to be used in a vertical format for street signs and in a horizontal format for other key communicators such as the canopy edge. Here the fluid "P" is stretched so it appears to swirl around the canopy and then to lick around the pump as a flash of red.

Petrol pumps on new forecourt

Close-up of pump

The pumps are incorporated into the structural columns to given an uncluttered appearance to the station forecourt. Stainless steel is used as a neutral but high-tech material to clad the columns, pump islands, kiosks and canopy edge. Stainless steel was specifically chosen since it is widely used in the Philippines and there are a large number of companies which supply it locally. It is also reminiscent of the brightly coloured and reflective Jeepneys made from the same material. Relics of the Second World War, these autos were left behind by the departing Americans, but they are still widely used today. Though Petron was keen to target the new middle classes, Jeepney drivers still represent a significant proportion of the market and it was important that they should not be alienated by the new designs.

Although in their designs Minale Tattersfield & Acton tried to use as much locally sourced material as possible, certain elements of the new identity required more high-tech machinery than could be provided locally without considerable investment. To combat this shortage, sign suppliers from developed markets were encouraged to invest in the Philippines. The arrangement proved beneficial to all involved since not only was Petron able to acquire top quality signs made using Western technology, but the investor was given the opportunity to exploit a significant new market and the local economy benefited from the investment.

station at night showing dramatic illumination

logo and interior of forecourt shop - Treats

Petron also recognised the importance of diversification given the reduced profit margins on fuel. To operate your own C-Store brand does, of course, ensure higher profit margins but it also requires a considerable initial investment in infrastructure. While some companies choose to invest in people to bring in the necessary expertise, others prefer to form an association with a partner brand which is already a specialist in the field. Petron decided on the former, calling their brand 'Treats' and it has proved a great success.

Final design of Petron station implemented across the network

Marcello Minale's comment

I have decided to include this project because I think it is one of the best examples of a design that has evolved from an existing corporate identity. The new "P" of Petron has strong links with the past but has successfully incorporated a graphic representation of movement, which is well suited to a company associated with transport.

It is also one of few brand identities where an interpretation of the symbol has been applied to the canopy to great effect.

13

brand identity and station design by
Minale Tattersfield & Acton for MTA Asia PTE

PETRONAS

brand identity and station design by Minale Tattersfield & Acton for MTA Design Asia

In 1995 Minale Tattersfield & Acton was commissioned by MTA Singapore to design a new station concept for the Petronas retail network. This was partly prompted by the multi-nationals, in particular Shell, BP and later Caltex, who were making considerable in-roads into the Malaysian market. Equally Petronas, as a state-owned company, had come to represent an outward expression of modern Malaysia. As such, it was important that the image it projected should represent modernity and dynamism and that it should not appear out of place alongside other global brands.

A new station design was just one manifestation of a larger brand push, clearly demonstrated by the building of the dramatic and graceful Petronas twin towers in Kuala Lumpur and the high profile tie-up with the glamorous world of Formula One.

It was decided to keep the corporate green for the retail network as it was sufficiently different to that of BP to avoid any confusion. It was also a cool and refreshing colour which worked well in the hot Malaysian climate. In addition, small flashes of magenta were introduced into the corporate palette for arrows on signage and to highlight information.

Petronas twin towers - Kuala Lumpur

Full view of new forecourt

Overhead signage of Petronas fuel pump

Whilst Petronas was keen to project a cutting edge image through its retail network, practical considerations also had to be taken into account. Most station refits are driven by cost and Petronas was no different. The technique used to light the canopy was particularly innovative and effective, yet extraordinarily simple. Standard Alucabond cladding panels are used with a white strip below. This is lit by green fluorescent tubes which wash green light along the canopy edge without the need for the normal backlighting materials of acrylic and vinyl, which incur increased cost and maintenance. In this way, the brand colour is highly visible both day and night. Since there are no panels to be removed when changing the neon strips, the solution allows very low maintenance.

Detail showing corner of canopy

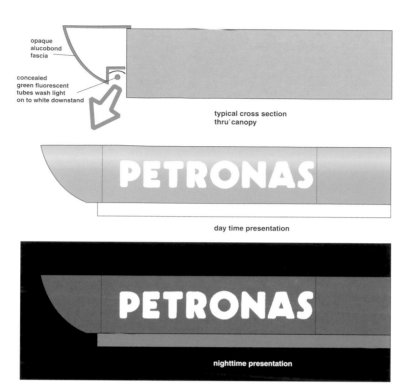

opaque
alucobond
fascia

concealed
green fluorescent
tubes wash light
on to white downstand

typical cross section
thru´canopy

PETRONAS

day time presentation

PETRONAS

nighttime presentation

Diagram illustrating the illumination of the canopy

Showing the underside of the canopy and lighting system

Old style of totem

New totem design

transportable petrol station

The Petronas carwash

Another clear demonstration of how Petronas is keen to stay abreast of the competition, by picking up on new ideas and technological advances, is the development of a concept for a cyber café. Designed to adjoin the C-Store, these are now being implemented. It appears that Petronas, unlike some of the major fuel retailers, has taken on board the importance of strong retail values and the need to provide customers with the level of service they have come to expect. In doing so they have continued to fly the Malaysian flag in style.

Marcello Minale's comment

Petronas is a company which occupies a special place in the heart of the Malaysian business community. I think that this project has demonstrated a clever implementation of the corporate colour and development of the existing identity. It is a very simple design which succeeds in conveying the company's premier position in the Malaysian business community.

The aqua blue is a unique and easy-to-remember colour and conveys the positive qualities of this very exciting nation.

14

corporate identity and station design by MTDS Paris
(Minale Tattersfield Design Strategy)

AFRIQUIA

corporate identity & station design by MTDS Paris (Minale Tattersfield Design Strateg

With its network of 170 petrol stations, Afriquia is the first national retailer to operate in Morocco. Their principal competitors are major international brands Shell and Total, which both operate networks of around 250 stations. Despite this, over the years Afriquia has developed strong customer loyalty and continues to expand, recently opening a further 15 new stations on the Ivory Coast. However, it is impossible to ignore the threat posed by these powerful market leaders which continue to operate an aggressive expansion policy. In response Afriquia has realised the importance of a strong and up-to-date brand identity and a comparable offer in terms of service. MTDS (Minale Tattersfield's French partners) was awarded the contract to design this new brand identity and a station concept which would help to maintain customer loyalty and meet competitors head on.

North Africa has not escaped the effects of reduced profit margins in the retail of petrol. So, as larger petrol retailers have begun to shift the emphasis away from the sale of petrol, diversifying their offer to make up for this loss, Afriquia is keen to follow suit. MTDS has designed a concept service centre which includes a central distribution area for petrol, a forecourt shop, a restaurant and a car repair centre. Each unit has been designed as a separate entity giving rise to franchise opportunities.

New identity - two-language version

Previous identity and design

New identity - single-language versions

A key factor in the design programme was that whilst Afriquia should be able to offer the same level of service as the international brands, their brand identity should be distinct. The existing station concept was a modified version of the ELF station, with white and blue stripes predominating. With its principal totem sign in white and the corporate identity a grey map of Africa against a red background, it failed to communicate any clear message and the overall effect was incoherent.

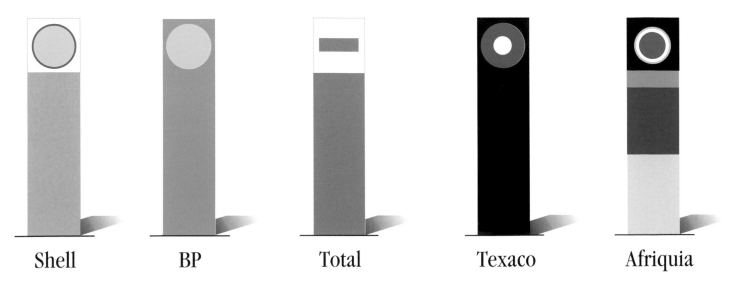

Shell   BP   Total   Texaco   Afriquia

Research showing competitors' colour distribution

development proposals for the canopy design

chosen design implemented on all new stations

Adaption of new design for retrofit stations

MTDS devised a brand identity and forecourt design which draws inspiration from North African heritage and immediately distinguishes Afriquia from competitors. Whereas many petrol retailers have opted for a generic station structure of simple cubic buildings and rectangular canopies supported by pillars, MTDS has designed an unusual sweeping station canopy which is unique to Afriquia. This dynamic wave design ensures the station is easily recognised at a distance. The station canopy is retained by supports which fulfil various functions: to group the pumps and to display signage and advertising. In this way, the various services on offer to the passing motorist are clearly indicated.

To complement this dynamic structure, MTDS decided a more fluid design would be appropriate for the corporate identity. Not only would this represent a move away from the static, heavy lettering favoured by many petrol retailers, but it would also reflect the energy and movement of the petrol industry. The new logo, which uses bright primary colours, is based on an abstract rendition of the African continent. Not immediately apparent to the eye, this symbol is a dynamic identity with an element of discovery.

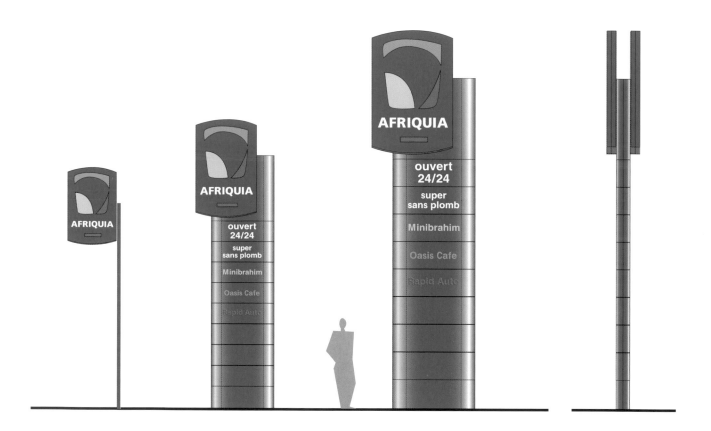

Family of totems

Arabic version of totem

French version of totem

The existing signage lacked visibility and MTDS advised a strong use of colour to rectify this. Blue was the obvious choice, as it is the dominant colour in the corporate palette and one that is not used by any of the major competitors. In sunny climates, such as Morocco, a strong use of colour is usually advisable as anything less can appear washed out. Since blue is not a particularly brilliant colour, the yellow, red and green of the corporate identity were also added for contrast. The totem is unusually shaped with the Afriquia logo offset and then outlined in red for greater impact.

ZONING STATION

CRÉATION
Principes de circulation et différents Accès

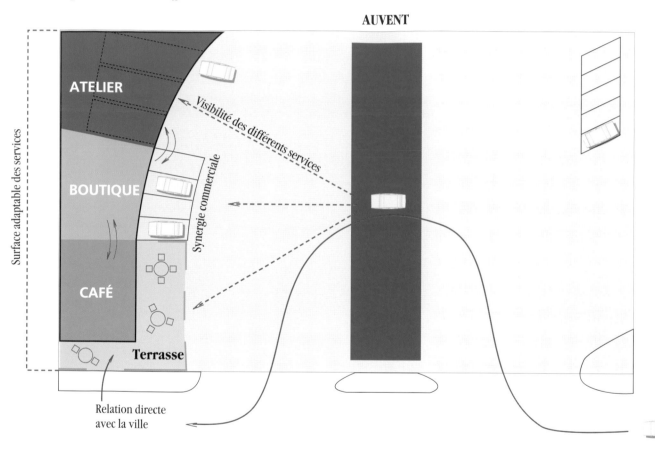

Plan of site showing traffic flow and location of café, shop and garage

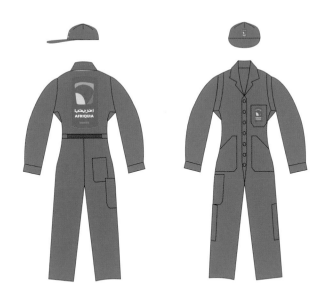

Uniforms for forecourt staff

The uniform in action!

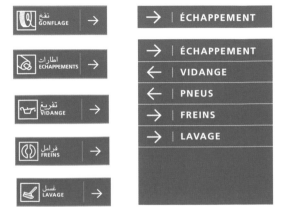

Signage for garage/maintenance area

The colours yellow, green and red have been carried through on the various offers. Each service building is clearly distinguished by colour, shape and a pattern applied to the building fascia. In this way the driver can see at a glance what services are available at each site without having to read any names.

The logotypes comprise illustrations which are easy to understand and the patterns used on the building fascias are reminiscent of decorations used in Moorish architecture.

The repair centre, Rapid'Auto, is red to represent speed with a motor-racing style chequered pattern. To ensure there is no confusion, the name is incorporated in a large screwdriver. The interior is spacious and welcoming.

A simplified version of this original concept is now being applied across the network.

Signage for Afriquia repair centre

Identity for repair centre

Design for Afriquia repair centre

Uniform for Rapid'Auto staff

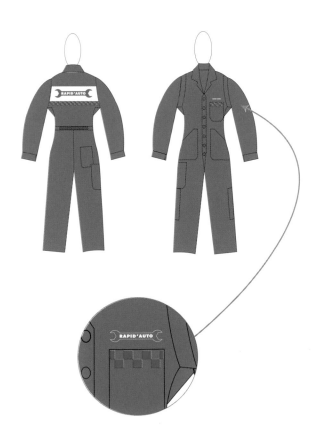

Identity for Afriquia's shop - Minibrahim

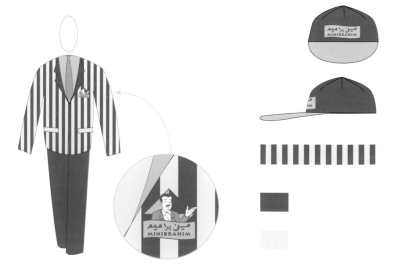

The logotype of the forecourt shop, Minibrahim, features a waiter. The building is yellow and its distinguishing pattern is that of yellow and blue stripes. The interior layout has been designed for self-service.

development drawing & photographs of implemented Minibrahim outlets

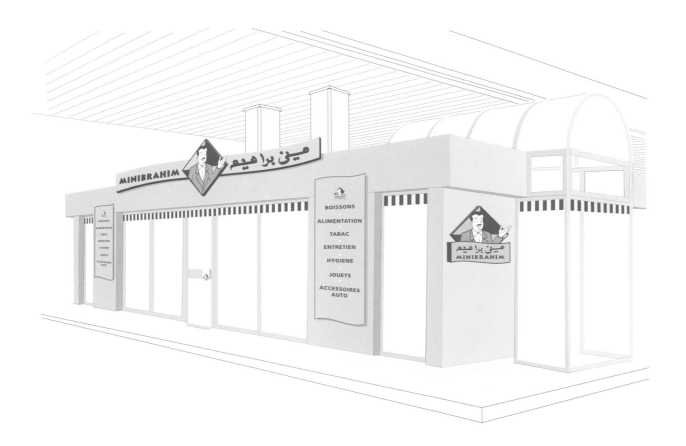

Identity for Afriquia's Oasis Café

The restaurant, branded Oasis Café, has a layout similar to that of a traditional Moorish house built around a central courtyard with a fountain. The building is designed as a green pyramid structure with a bar at its centre and a large adjoining terrace with a central fountain. Its distinguishing pattern is a traditional and distinctive diamond pattern.

Architectural proposal for Oasis Café

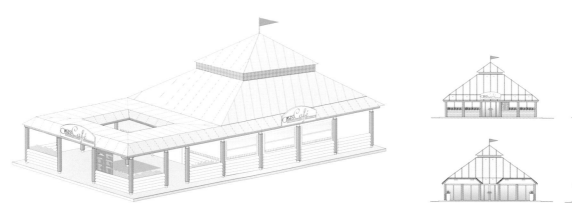

Perspective and end views of Oasis Café

Oasis Café above a Minibrahim shop

Final design of Afriquia station at night, incorporating Rapid'Auto and Minibrahim convenience store

Marcello Minale's comment

This is the first non-linear canopy to be successfully produced on an industrial scale. The design is such that it can be constructed on site by local workers, as opposed to in the factory.

The wave canopy is an ideal shape for a hot climate since it creates an area of cool and aids ventilation. Let's not forget that temperatures in Morocco often soar to above 45°. Full credit to our French partners!

15

Agip designed by Minale Tattersfield & Acton
Mintat G3 designed by Minale Tattersfield Design Strategy

MINTAT G3 TRANSPORTABLE PETROL STATION
Agip station designed by Minale Tattersfield & Acton
Mintat G3 designed by Minale Tattersfield Design Strategy

The concept was first conceived by Marcello Minale while on a trip to Russia. He saw that people were driving miles to refuel from makeshift stations or jerry cans at the side of the road. He felt that an innovative concept was needed to address the problem.

The original station was designed by Minale Tattersfield & Acton in collaboration with AGIP. Although it was not the first transportable petrol station to be produced, the AGIP transportable petrol station was the first to be built on a modular system based on standard international shipping containers. A prototype was constructed and tested in Prague. It was intended for use in developing economies where existing re-fuelling infrastructures were inadequate to cope with increased demand from consumers, or where tightening regulations restricted the building of permanent stations.

A model of the final AGIP transportable petrol station design

However, research revealed further possible applications of the station. This included use in remote areas where consumers were being forced to pay a higher price for fuel or where retailers were being subsidised. The transportable petrol station could provide the solution since it requires less investment than a permanent station and can be unmanned to reduce overheads. It is also suited to use in areas where there is considerable fluctuation in population such as popular holiday destinations or large sporting events and festivals. Equally it can serve as an alternative supply when petrol stations are being refurbished to reduce loss of revenue.

Furthermore, we also realised that with the exploration of alternative fuels to petrol and diesel, success would depend on a good re-fuelling infrastructure for the new fuel. One of the major factors in the development of hybrid powered vehicles, such as LPG (liquid petroleum gas) and electrical engines, would be a good re-fuelling infrastructure. If this infrastructure is mobile it reduces the cost and time of implementation.

In 1999, following the testing of the Prague prototype, Frank van der Zwan, an MSc student from Delft University, conducted a feasibility study of the transportable petrol station. His findings are included in the following report:

MARKET RESEARCH ON THE MINTAT STATION
by Frank van der Zwan taken from his MSc Industrial Design Engineering thesis
at Delft University of Technology, Holland
sponsored by Minale Tattersfield Design Strategy

History of Mintat station

Minale Tattersfield & Acton began work on the transportable petrol station project in 1995. The idea came to Marcello Minale when, on a trip to Moscow, he was surprised to see people selling petrol from make-shift cabins along the roadside. On his return he approached AGIP (due to their strong presence in the Eastern Bloc) with a view to developing a transportable petrol station. This resulted in the Prague prototype which was installed in 1987.

The concept of a transportable petrol station itself was not new. The innovation lay in the fact that it was based on a modular system. There were additional pragmatic reasons for building a non-permanent structure as a means of avoiding the complicated bureaucracy common in Eastern Bloc countries. Equally, Minale Tattersfield wanted to build a station which would match the stylish cars that used it. An important element of the concept was that different corporate identities could be applied to it.

Having installed the prototype, AGIP decided not to proceed with the project since it wanted to stick to what it does best - selling petrol! Minale Tattersfield decided to proceed independently, but since AGIP kept the prototype and all the technical information*, it was necessary to start from scratch. For this next concept Minale Tattersfield consulted CKT, a specialist in production engineering based in Rotterdam. This resulted in the Mintat G1, a concept which looked like the Prague prototype but which was built to meet UK legislative standards.

After this, the concept was extended with additional units such as extra pumps, tanks and a separator. The need to develop a station that was as cost-effective as possible led to a re-evaluation of the layout and resulted in the Mintat G2, a concept where all the fuel storage and dispensing equipment is put in one container. To reduce costs further the ramps have been taken away and greater emphasis has been placed on on-site preparation, which now includes a separator and drainage system as well as electricity, running water and sewage disposal.

* Subsequently Agip has released all technical drawings and licence
  to produce the station, to Minale Tattersfield & Partners.

Front and side views

Background to research

Having developed the Prague prototype, Minale Tattersfield believed it had a useful concept which could provide a solution for various specific needs of clients across the world. Thus far it had been acting on its own judgement and experience, but there were still had many questions concerning issues such as price and safety regulations, as well as the final design. Therefore,   a more strategic and systematic approach was needed.

Minale Tattersfield set up a project to undertake market research into the petrol station market. The aims of the research would be a thorough market description of a number of fruitful and characteristic geographical markets, a regulation report on the Mintat station for these markets and suggestions for design refinements of the Mintat concept.

Market Analysis

The goal of the analysis was to give Minale Tattersfield a better understanding of the potential of the Mintat station.

First of all, the different uses of the Mintat station had to be understood, since these uses would generate different requirements of the station. Descriptions of some of the possible applications of the station follow:

• in cases of environmental constraint - providing fuel in areas where there is a demand but where environmental constraints do not allow traditional stations to be built

• in rural areas - providing fuel in areas with low population density that do not justify the large scale investment of a permanent station

• during refurbishment - providing fuel and other services when main outlets are refurbished

• as temporary additional fuel sales points - providing additional fuel dispensers in areas with large seasonal fluctuations in population (eg during vacation periods at holiday destinations)

• during special events - providing fuel at unusual places for a short time, eg during trade fairs and sporting events

• where there is a need for extra infrastructure - providing fuel where conventional stations have not yet been built

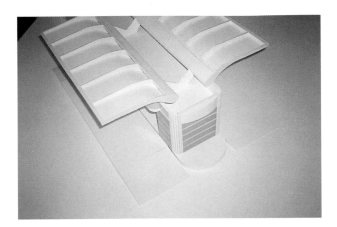

First stages of making the transportable petrol station model

Every application illustrates certain desired characteristics. When the Mintat station is used in rural areas, for example, the costs need to be considerably lower than that of a conventional station in order for the Mintat station to be a viable option. The station should also be suitable for conversion into a compact unmanned station to keep operating costs low. However, when the station is going to be used during special events, its non-permanent character and ease of operation are the important qualities. By looking at the different uses of the Mintat station, a first set of desired characteristics or requirements can be established.

To gain further insight into the global potential of the Mintat station, research in countries around the world needed to be carried out, since every country has its own geographical characteristics, types of fuel and safety regulations. Conducting research on about 200 countries was not feasible, so a selection had to made. The following "key" countries were chosen as a representative sample because they are a major interest and have varied geographies: Germany, South Africa, and the United States of America. During the analysis several types of data were studied. Geo- and demographic data, economic data, petrol station market data and station costs estimates - all to get an understanding of the 'environment' (in its broadest sense) in which the station might be placed.

Germany

Germany is a temperate country with no extremes in geographical or climatological conditions. It is still one of the wealthiest countries in Europe despite the richer West Germany having carried the burden of the poorer East for the last 10 years. Petrol station networks in Germany, as in most Western European countries, are decreasing. The main reason is profitability; smaller and less economic sites are closed down and the prime sites are improved. This has consequences for the possible uses of the Mintat station. The station is most likely to be used during refurbishment of the main outlets. As is the case when the station is used for events, the non-permanent character of the station is important.

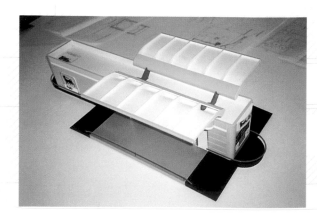

Development of transportable petrol station model

South Africa

The petrol station market in South Africa is relatively small; there are only four to seven large petrol-retailing companies. The number of petrol stations is steadily growing. The South African government wants to stimulate the development of small petrol stations, generating work for local people and enabling minor petrol retailers to participate fully in the petrol market. The Mintat station can fulfill this need by providing an easy and standardised way of expanding the networks. The costs of fuel and of building standard 'bricks-and-mortar' stations in South Africa is low compared to that of Western European countries, so it is not economically viable to import the station into the country from Europe. Local companies would have to be found to manufacture the station within South Africa.

United States of America

According to the Journal of Petroleum Marketing, (1998), there are over 180,000 retail facilities selling motor fuels in the United States. This makes the USA by far the largest petrol station market in the world (in comparison there are 17,000 in Germany, 4,800 in South Africa). There are about 8,000 companies that operate more than one petrol station each 1,000 operating 20 or more stations. This means there is a large potential market for the Mintat station in the USA. The United States consists of 50 states, each subdivided into counties and cities. Each state is free to adopt its own legislation, and in some of the states even county and city governments are free to adopt their own standards. This could make entering the United States a difficult and time-consuming endeavour.

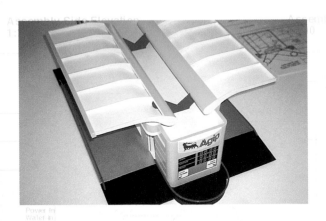

Conclusions from market analysis

The analysis clearly shows that the petrol station 'environment' in every country is different. The different applications of the station need to be taken into account to make sure that the Mintat station is actually fit for its proposed purpose. The non-permanent character of the station, for example, seems to be important for several of its possible uses.

Final transportable petrol station model for AGIP

Fire and safety regulations study

Petrol is a highly flammable and toxic liquid and is therefore subjected to a plethora of regulations. These regulations prescribe the planning and design of the petrol station, including the location of tanks and pipelines, as well as the construction and installation of metering pumps and dispensers and the storage of fuel in the tanks. Almost all codes and regulations have a clause like that of the US Automotive and Marine Service Station Code provided by the National Fire Protection Agency (NFPA):

"These codes are recommended for use as the basis for legal regulations. Its provisions are intended to reduce the hazard to a degree consistent with reasonable public safety...Nothing in this code is intended to prevent the use of systems, methods, or devices of equivalent or superior quality, strength, fire resistance, effectiveness, durability and safety over those prescribed..." (NFPA 30A, art.1-4)

This leaves space for unconventional petrol stations, like the Mintat station, "provided technical documentation is submitted...to demonstrate equivalency and provided the system, method or device is approved for the intended purpose." (NFPA 30A, art.1-4)

Since the Mintat station is a novel design, it is important to understand to what degree the station meets the fire and safety regulations in the researched countries and what problems there might be meeting them. To gain this understanding, the legislation and codes of practice of the three countries have been investigated.

The main departures of the Mintat station from the regulations are the aboveground instead of underground fuel storage, the relatively small distance between the fuel tank and the fuel dispensers, the small distance between the fuel dispensers and the shop and the connection of the fuel storage tank to the surface of the site. These departures have been taken into account during the refinement stage.

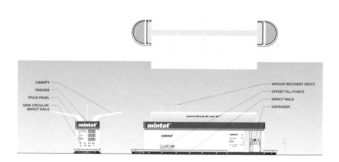

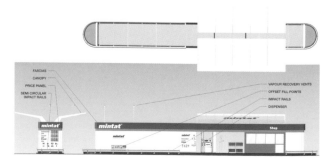

Ancap prototype

Above - the basic G3 unit, below - G3 with retail unit

Refining of the concept

This section introduces only a few of the many conclusions drawn from the full market analysis conducted. Generally these conclusions fell into two groups: aspects that have not yet been specified and physical weaknesses of the concept.

It seems reasonable that the most useful conclusions for refinement of the concept were the ones of the latter type. Therefore, the following suggestions for refining the concept have been made:

• optimise the fuel dispensing unit for use as an independent unit, look into the changes that need to be made to convert the unit into an unmanned station

• ensure the non-permanent character of the station, but also look into the anchoring of the station to secure a rigid and safe station

• develop concepts for increased fuel storage capacity and shop size compared to the existing concept

• develop concepts which have adjustable separation distances between the fuel dispensers and shop, and fuel dispensers and tank

Conclusions

The market analysis has resulted in increased knowledge of the potential markets of the Mintat station.

The regulations and applications studies have identified the desired characteristics and shown the current weaknesses of the Mintat station concept.

This project has been used to improve the Mintat station and the outcome is a much more viable petrol station.

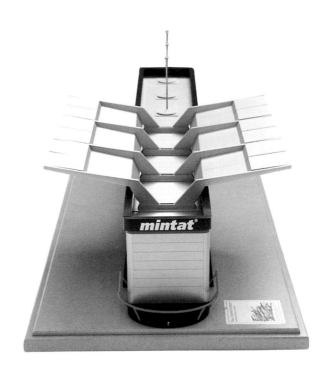

Mintat G3

mintat G3

Based on the findings of van der Zwan's report, the original concept station, developed in 1995, was modified and updated to produce the latest model, the Mintat G3, which now meets stringent European safety standards. The station is built on a flexible modular system of inter-connectable units, the basic model being split into three compartments. The tank section is based on 12m international standard steel shipping containers whilst the shop section can comprise either 6m, 9m or 12m modules which ensures the unit is adaptable for various site sizes and facilities. These units provide durability and ease of transportation and installation. It is an economical, rapid response solution and can be installed and operational within 48 hours, holding up to 30,000 litres of fuel. Being easy to transport, this modular system is also ideal for use in the event of natural disasters limiting access to isolated areas, or for market testing of demand for new products and locations.

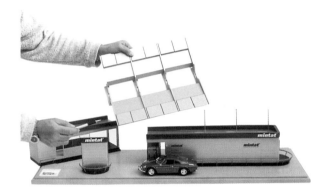

Minale demonstrating the modular system

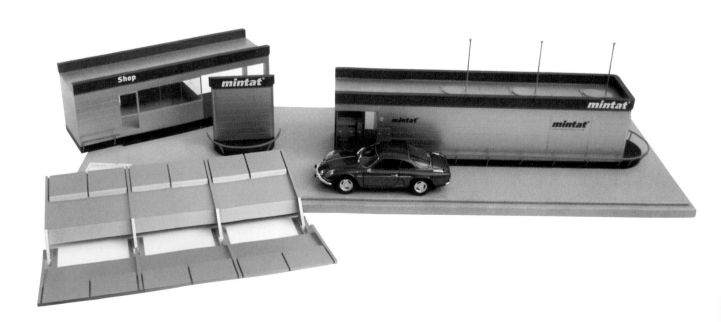

Close up view of the Mintat G3 showing petrol pumps

Since the Mintat G3, produced by Maser, is not a mass produced item the design can be adapted to a client's particular requirements. It is very easy to have the unit fully automated for unmanned operation, to include photo-voltaic cells, a roadside café section and so on.

The project has received enormous interest from all over the world: from oil companies, armies and governments, to name but a few. And Minale Tattersfield continues to refine the design in order to reduce further production costs and to improve an already very high level of safety.

Final version of the complete station

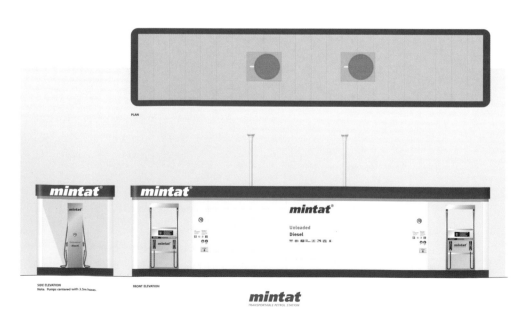

A twin pump version (to service four cars) of the Mintat G3 station

Marcello Minale's comment

The Mintat G3 is an evolution of the AGIP station. The design is more flexible as the main body has all the requirements for a retail operation. As profits increase additional features can be added such as a shop unit, wings or rails.

Not only is this station suited for use in areas under reconstruction following conflicts or natural disasters, but it has the look of a sophisticated and technologically advanced dispensing unit which is appropriate for use outside supermarkets and in other urban locations.

We all know that at present European legislation does not allow the tank to be located above ground. However there is currently a movement in the Swedish Parliament to legislate for future petrol stations to be built with tanks above ground for ecological reasons. Should this come about, there will be an explosion in the use of transportable petrol stations. I believe that the authorities have not really been challenged to reassess the situation so that this type of station can be legalised. The Mintat G3 is in a good position to achieve this aim.

16

identity and 3D design by
Minale Tattersfield Design Strategy

MASER

identity & 3D design by Minale Tattersfield Design Strategy

Maser is an Italian company which for the last ten years has specialised in the development and manufacture of automated systems for the oil sector. Based outside Bologna, they continue to expand their operations and in 1999 they commissioned Minale Tattersfield & Partners to update their brand identity in order to reinforce their position as a technologically advanced and dynamic market leader. In addition, Minale Tattersfield was to design new shells for their two forecourt automated pay systems, the MAC and MAF, to be relaunched in 2000.

Previous identity

Initial development of existing logo

Development of new logo - various colour combinations

Final logo proposal

The new brand is reminiscent of the style used by the automotive industry and reflects the advanced technology and precision engineering on which Maser has built its reputation. "The typographical style of the original logo had become outdated", remarks Minale Tattersfield's 3D Design Director, Peter Brown. "We began by modernising it to look more like a car brand to judge how far the client was willing to go, but in the end we were able to adopt a more radical approach." The new identity is in the style of a car badge and retains the corporate green. It uses a more modern typeface and incorporates a stylised graphic representation of the petrol pump, which also suggests Maser's broad ranging expertise and the wide variety of products it has developed for all areas of the oil industry. These elements introduce a chromium colour into the identity which appears to reflect the light, giving a high quality finish.

SOLUZIONE PER L'AUTOMAZIONE

Maser s.p.a.
Via dell'Industria 40
40064 Ozzano Emilia (Bo)
Italia
T.+39 51 791711
F. +39 51 791718
E. maser@internetbusiness.it
www.maserworld.com

SOLUZIONE PER L'AUTOMAZIONE

Giuseppe Berardo
Direttore Generale

Maser s.p.a.
Via dell'Industria 40
40064 Ozzano Emilia (Bo)
Italia
T. +39 51 791711
F. +39 51 791718
E. maser@internetbusiness.it
www.maserworld.com

Logo applied to stationary

initial design proposals for payment terminals

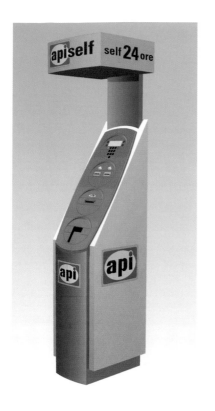

Concept A

Concept B

Concept C

examples of petrol company branding on concepts B & C

development of form of MAC unit

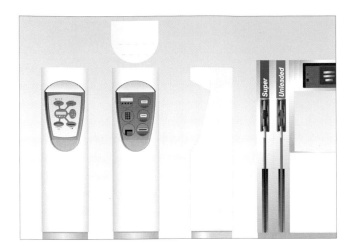

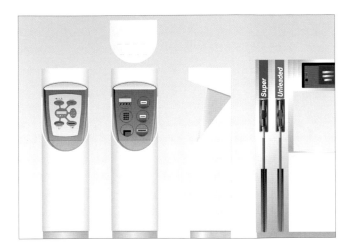

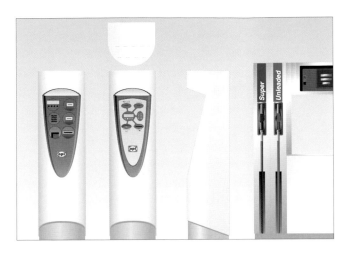

The new shells for the two automated payment systems have been designed to complement the new brand identity. The MAF is a simple card payment system whilst the MAC includes a banknote reader and safe. An important consideration which influenced the design solution was the need to integrate the instrument panel better so as to improve the series of functions for use through better grouping.

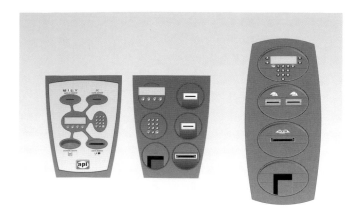

Consoles from original proposals

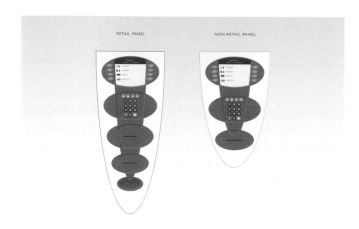

Console development for MAC and MAF units

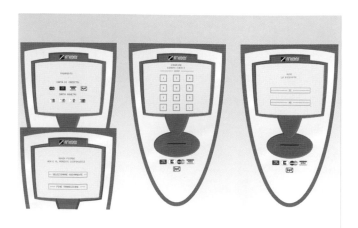

Example of touchscreen interfaces for MAF units

Three development concepts were produced. The first design incorporates a simple vertical interface and in style it reflects a petrol pump. The second, with the circular detailing of the interface, not only isolates the different functions but also reflects a car instrument panel. The third design comprises a curved front which echoes the curves of the logo and uses an interface which playfully groups the elements, whilst also creating a logical sequence of use.

Provisions were made for an optional, changeable metal panel for the console which provides flexibility to alter its appearance and creates a high quality finish. Although this was popular, the idea was dropped due to the additional expense it would incur. In addition to the standard key pad and screen option, the alternative touch screen system with a larger full colour screen was also considered. However, in the end Maser opted for the curved fronted shell with the vertical, key pad operated interface. To integrate this, the shape of the shell was elongated which created a more elegant appearance as a result.

This formula was then adapted to the various models, including a wall mounted version.

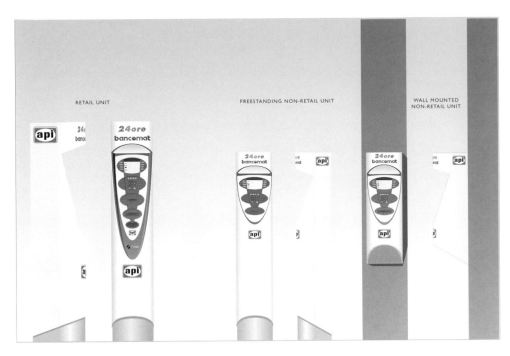

Development of family of pay terminals

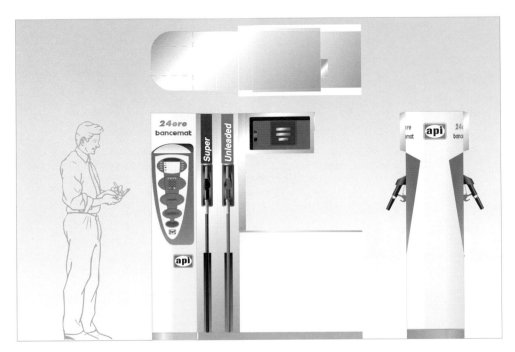

Retrofit proposal for pay terminals

Final console

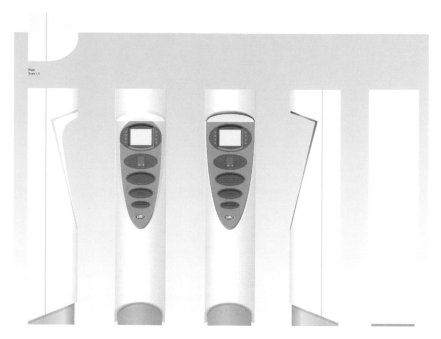

Final proposal for pay terminals

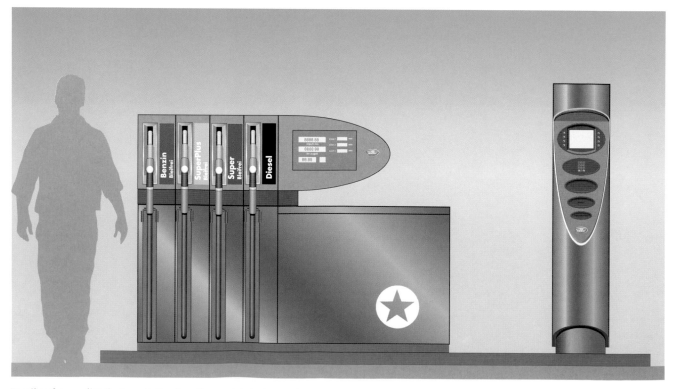

Family of new distributor - following the same design style

Marcello Minale's comment

This project represented a challenge for us since, though well versed in most aspects of forecourt design, it was the first time we had designed an automatic payment unit. It is now under construction and will be launched in Frankfurt in September 2000.

The design looks promising. We have succeeded in bringing a more dynamic, automotive-style shape to a static machine for the first time.

17

architect: Eric R. Kuhne Associates
corporate identity designed by Minale Tattersfield Design Strategy
sign system designed by Minale Tattersfield Bryce

BLUEWATER

architect: Eric R. Kuhne Associates
corporate identity designed by Minale Tattersfield Design Strategy
sign system designed by Minale Tattersfield Bryce

In 1995 Minale Tattersfield Bryce was commissioned by Lend Lease Global Investments to create an identity for a vast new shopping complex, which was to open in Kent.

Bluewater is the largest shopping complex of its kind in Europe. Designed by Eric Kuhne, it ingeniously combines both retail shopping and leisure.

The shopping centre, which is built in a disused chalk quarry, aimed to create the atmosphere of a medieval village located in a hidden valley.

The chosen design for the corporate identity, depicts a rampant horse leaping from the water. The symbolic representation of the Invicta horse of Kent gives a historical perspective and the image reflects its geographic location.

Bluewater is surrounded by water - the new chalk pit lakes, the Thames Estuary and the North Sea are all close by. On visiting the complex, shoppers are aware of these expanses of water, thus reinforcing the Bluewater name and visual identity.

Minale Tattersfield was subsequently commissioned to design concepts for signage, including traffic, pedestrian, building and architectural signage. A system of colour coding and visual themes facilitates easy orientation around the vast complex.

External view of Bluewater

The Bluewater logo - designed by Minale Tattersfield Design Strategy

View of the interior of the mall

View of the interior of the mall showing heraldic banners

Proposal for sign system

Indoor signage

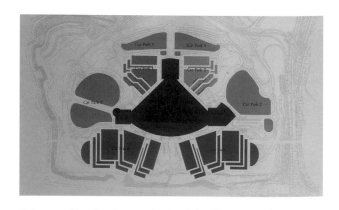

Colour-coding for the precincts of the Bluewater site

Marcello Minale's comment

Bluewater is not an 'Energy Project' but we have included it in this book because it is probably the best assembly of 'convenience stores' (300 of them). The petrol industry can learn from this example, letting the public see what they want before they spend their money!

Bluewater also has a good sign system programme which is very important for the gas station.

It goes without saying that the architect Eric R. Kuhne, the Master of Grandiose, has produced a space that works and entertains at the same time.

18

name, branding and interiors designed by
Minale Tattersfield Design Strategy

THE REFINERY

name, branding and interiors designed by Minale Tattersfield Design Strategy

To finish off we have a twist to the tale. Though at first glance this project may appear closely associated to the subject of petrol stations, The Refinery shares nothing with the oil industry except its name. It is in fact a top quality grooming salon for men which has recently opened in London. So why include it? To illustrate how in recent years preconceptions have changed to such a degree that The Refinery has become an acceptable brand name for a grooming salon! Petrol stations have come a long way from the dirty, greasy, uninviting places they used to be.

The male grooming industry may be booming on the Continent and in the States, but it is only just beginning to take off here in the UK. All this is set to change, however, with the opening of The Refinery, a state-of-the-art, one-stop day spa for men. And whilst it offers top of the range treatments in luxurious surroundings, its aim is to be neither exclusive nor prohibitively expensive.

The name The Refinery has both industrial and cleansing connotations. For many the word 'Refinery' conjures up images of the male dominated world of heavy industry. But the process of removing impurities or defects could, of course, apply to any good haircut or facial.

Identity for London's premier grooming emporium for men!

reception area, hair salon and changing room

The double meaning of the name is captured in Minale Tattersfield's logo. Drawn in the style of a hand-written signature, it resembles a small oil slick or looks as though it has been poured from molten metal. The industrial nature of refining oils and metals is emphasised by the metallic feel of the lettering whilst the hand-written style signifies the personal contact so important in the leisure and service industries.

Situated just off Bond Street, the location for the flagship spa is ideal in appealing to a broad cross section of the male population - on the borders of the cross-over between old money and new money and a destination area for style-conscious men of all economic groups.

vichy shower treatment room, lounge area and reception

Built in a five-storey classic Georgian townhouse, the primary concern was that the interior should be in sympathy with the building itself whilst fulfilling its purpose as a modern-day grooming sanctuary. On top of this, it was important it should have a broad appeal without forgoing a level of sophistication and aspirational style likely to appeal to potential customers. And since your average British male might need some reassurance that indulging in a bit of pampering does not question his masculinity, an unpretentious and accessible atmosphere was going to be a key factor in the success of the project.

The building lends itself to the traditional style of a gentleman's club but so as to avoid an atmosphere of stuffiness, a contemporary angle was adopted. The materials used are natural and traditional but used in a contemporary context. Dark oak doors, marble floors, granite tiling and stone-coloured, ivory or deep blue walls work together to create an environment which is at the same time luxurious and stylish.

Range of packaging for The Refinery

Marcello Minale's comment

A trendy grooming salon for men in fashionable London being called The Refinery. What greater indication could there be that the petrol station has been transformed from the uneco-friendly and unhealthy place of former years to a clean and welcoming spot offering a valuable service to the community

various petrol stations...

Every designer, before starting a new project must research the market. Here is a collage of various stations - some well designed, some not, but each an inspiration!

MINALE TATTERSFIELD DESIGN STRATEGY GROUP

Minale Tattersfield & Partners, UK (HEAD OFFICE)
The Courtyard, 37 Sheen Road
Richmond, Surrey TW9 1AJ
Tel: +44 (0)20 8948 7999 Fax: +44 (0)20 8948 2435
ISDN: +44 (0)20 8332 2160 Email: mtp@mintat.co.uk
www.mintat.co.uk

MTDS (Minale Tattersfield Design Strategy), FRANCE
192 avenue Charles de Gaulle
92200 Neuilly-sur-Seine, France
Tel: +33 1 41 92 97 00 Fax: +33 1 41 92 97 01
Email:mtds@wandadoo.fr

Minale Tattersfield Italia, MILAN
Largo V Alpini 8, 20123 Milano, Italy
Tel: +39 02 480 100 87 Fax: +39 02 480 082 08
Email: minale@spacetwo.wirenet.it
www.mintat.it

Minale Tattersfield Bryce & Partners Pty Ltd. BRISBANE
212 Boundary Street, Spring Hill, Brisbane Qld 4000, Australia
Tel: +61 7 3831 4149 Fax: +61 7 3832 1653
Email: brisbane@mtbdesign.com.au

Minale Tattersfield Piaton & Partners, BUENOS AIRES
Maipú 859, 1006 Buenos Aires, Argentina
Tel: +54 1 314 62 62 Fax: +54 1 314 77 30
Email: stef@step.net.ar

* Minale Tattersfield & Partners or any other company of the Minale Tattersfield Design Strategy Group are in no way associated with MTA Design

the end